T0368330

LIFE, DEATH, THE UNIVERSE, AND SOME OTHER STUFF

JOHN C. HEGLIN

AuthorHouse™
1663 Liberty Drive
Bloomington, IN 47403
www.authorhouse.com
Phone: 833-262-8899

*Because of the dynamic nature of the Internet, any web addresses or links contained in this book may have changed
since publication and may no longer be valid. The views expressed in this work are solely those of the author and do not
necessarily reflect the views of the publisher, and the publisher hereby disclaims any responsibility for them.*

*Any people depicted in stock imagery provided by Getty Images are models,
and such images are being used for illustrative purposes only.
Certain stock imagery © Getty Images.*

This book is printed on acid-free paper.

ISBN: 978-1-6655-7581-2 (sc)
ISBN: 978-1-6655-7582-9 (e)

Print information available on the last page.

Published by AuthorHouse 11/23/2022

authorHOUSE®

To Arlene, Barby, and Connie, the people who believed
I could write before I believed it myself.

Contents

About the Author

John C. Heglin was born in Florida, but grew up in the San Fernando Valley near L.A. When he was thirteen, he moved with his family to the San Diego area, to which he has returned periodically amid numerous world-traveling adventures, experiencing life from being homeless to well-heeled.

As a student of psychology, he attended both the University of San Diego and Grossmont College, where he also taught for a time.

JCH in author's Russian dance suite

Still going strong in his sixth decade, John has been a professional dancer / choreographer and educator his whole life. He taught grade levels from first grade through college.

However, to supplement that income, he has also been a working counselor, a jeweler, an architectural model builder, has worked in the heart of nuclear reactors, has rebuilt houses, and been a merchant marine. He is an award-winning artist whose work has been displayed in museums, and an award-winning patented inventor.

His adventurous spirit led him to climb some of the highest peaks on the continent solo, swim in the sea more than a hundred miles from any land, take the controls of a plane high above the earth, and clamber alone through caves deep within it.

He is now an over-worked apple farmer during his "retirement," living with his "Wonder Muffin" Arlene, fifteen chickens, and a pet chinchilla.

Foreword

I was profoundly lonely as a young teen when my sister dragged me to a folk dance in Balboa Park, insisting there was someone I had to know. That someone was John Heglin, with his confident dancer's posture, shock of curly blonde hair and piercing blue eyes that saw to the core of my being. From the moment he took my sweaty hand on that warm summer night to guide me onto the dance floor, we were soul mates. Sadly, my sister has long since disappeared from our lives. But I thank her; she could not have been more insightful. Although we lost her, we were no longer alone. Through more years than I will admit, John and I have remained as close as that first glorious, floor-grazing waltz—no matter how many miles life has wedged between us.

Through the years we shared our daily stories in person or by phone--from miserable, to tragic, to joyful. His background in psychology, combined with an astonishing capacity for love, proved him to be an empathetic, tireless and very wise listener. Sharing trauma-filled childhoods, the union of our spirits allowed us to forge an invincible capacity to transform turmoil into tranquility and heartbreak into laughter. No matter how hard the world pushes against us, our connection is always more powerful.

Without John, I would not be here.

But I assure you, he was not one to simply sit back and listen. He was also a delightful raconteur with a deceptively easy style that would catch me off guard every time. As you will discover, his stories are wildly amusing and captivating. Those of us who have been fortunate to hear him tell these stories encouraged him to commit them to the printed word.

I am happy to say that I experienced many of his stories in this book first hand. I knew him shortly after his early childhood stories when they were still fresh in his mind and I bore witness to the later ones, usually within hours of their occurrence. I assure you, they are wild, weird, and sometimes insane--and all are true. With the wit and richly complex narrative of Mark Twain and the folksy narrative vigor of Garrison Keillor, I personally choose to read these stories one at a time, so I can savor every moment. Inevitably, each story leaves me hungry for the next adventure.

Barbara Rose: Award-winning Multimedia Producer/Director, Writer, Director of Development Film/TV, Producer of RacigNellieBly.com and graduate in English and Comparative Literature.

Preface

It was a dark and stormy night the night I was born.

Well, at least it must have been somewhere, this is a big planet after all. As for the weather in the little seaside Florida town I was born in, I have no idea. You see, I was very young when I was born, and I can't say as I remember.

Author on High

I have been told that I needed to write a preface. This is something I've never done or even tried to do before. However, I shall endeavor to try to do so now.

Already I am uncomfortable with the number of times I have written the word "I." Although, seeing as these are all actual stories about my actual life, I guess it is somewhat appropriate. About these stories, I can only say that they are all true, and as absolutely accurate as humanly possible. As an indication of the sincerity of my attempt at accuracy, the reader may notice a general lack of dialogue. This is because although I, at this point, have a very clear recollection of the pertinent events, I am not as certain of what was word for word said, and by whom, and I wouldn't want to falsely put words in anyone's mouth.

I would also like to apologize up front for a certain amount of redundancies present between some of the stories. These offerings were, in fact, written to be individual stories, and stand on their own. Therefore, some of the necessary background setup will seem familiar to the reader persistent enough to make their way through more than a few of my adventures.

As for the stories, again, they are my true-life experiences. After relating some of these adventures to friends on various social occasions, said friends implored me to record them in a more permanent fashion. Only after repeated and insistent cajoling did I reluctantly acquiesce to putting pen to paper. Or, more accurately, putting fingers to keyboard.

My origin could be accurately, although speaking figuratively, described as dark and stormy. Due to a confluence of unfortunate circumstances, I was unloved and unwanted from birth. Many feel this way, but my feelings were solidly confirmed when I accidentally overheard a conversation between my parents and my shocked and incredulous uncle wherein they laid out the whole unfortunate story. Hey, what are the chances huh? And, I know, I know, "woe is me!" This is not a complaint, however, nor is it the general tone of this book, just a part of my former reality.

Perhaps at some later time I'll relate that small novel, but that is not what these stories are about. In fact, if anything, that situation made the circumstances that led to many of these stories possible. You see, unwanted translates to largely unsupervised, and unsupervised leaves one open to opportunities for exploration and adventure. Exploration and adventure often lead to self-sufficiency and endless curiosity, and oh how that formula worked on me!

I have always wanted to know everything about everything. About science and nature and history and humanity and love, especially love, something I knew so little of throughout my early life. Unlike most people, I learned about love through logic and reason, and that has served me remarkably well in life, so far. I have found within myself a tremendous capacity to love, and accept love from others.

And death! I was curious as hell about death. So far, I have, through no fault of my own, had the dubious good fortune to have been technically dead, heart stopped and all that, on four separate occasions. Cool huh? People have said, and I have found this to be true, that the best way to learn about something is to do it. I guess I may have to write about that someday as well.

Until then, I have but these few humble stories to offer. And with them my hope that they may inspire you, dear reader, to find your own personal curiosity about Life, Death, The Universe, and Some Other Stuff.

How Bugs Bunny Saved my Life

It may sound hard to believe to some, but it is nevertheless true, that were it not for Bugs Bunny (yes, the cartoon "wascally wabbit"), I would not be here to relate this story.

It must have been late summer of 1964, just before school started. It took place in Placerita Canyon, just north of the San Fernando Valley in the Angeles National Forest, at a primitive campground with only about five camp sites consisting of a picnic table and a fire ring. The whole campground had one water spigot and what must have been some kind of outhouse.

I first learned about the campground while attending a nearby, not to be named, Christian camp for young boys, whose goal it was to indoctrinate said boys while they were young and impressionable. The attempt failed in my case due to the unconscionable and, in my innocent young mind, contradictory behavior of the camp leaders who would force the kids to listen to Bible stories before they would allow them to eat their lunch. And then, after lunch, lead the kids out into nature to find some small helpless animal to kill with rocks and sticks!

However, my brother Jim and I had learned from the experience that we liked camping. We later managed to convince our father to take us camping at Placerita on one occasion, and to drop us off there with some of the neighborhood kids, a few being older, on another occasion.

The campground was a great place for us kids, especially when left unsupervised. The location was quite remote, yet only less than ten miles from my home in the valley. The area, at that time, was much undeveloped, so we had the feeling we were far away in the great western outdoors. We would spend the days running around, shooting each other with BB guns, cooking and eating hot dogs over a campfire, catching little frogs in the mere trickle of a stream and sneaking them into someone's canteen when they weren't looking, catching lizards, and mostly hiking and finding and exploring some of the numerous abandoned old gold mines that pockmarked the whole area. After all, the name Placerita refers to the placer gold deposits that were the cause of a minor gold rush there a hundred years before.

It was a place filled with fun, history and real adventure.

Well, to the story at hand.

On that late summer occasion, as the specter of school threatened to lock us kids indoors for most of our coming days, I had the brilliant idea of a camp-out. The idea was very well received and in no time, I had four or five other kids on-board, had received parental permission and convinced my father to drive us out there the next day. Wow, was this going to be fun!

However, no sooner had I begun gathering my supplies, than one by one, everyone started to bail on me.

I won't go into their various excuses except to say that they were all pretty lame and left me with the distinct impression that they were all scared. This could have been because the last time we camped there we were kept awake most of the night by, what was probably a pack rat, making thrashing noises in the bushes just a few feet away. I must admit even I was spooked by what we kept kidding each other was a bear or a lion or some horrible alien monster looking to snack on human children. Kids, with imaginations, on their own, in the dark?

The upshot is, by the next day, everyone, even my brother, had backed out on me.

Now, at this point, a smart kid would admit defeat. A kid of the world would look at it philosophically and say, "There will be other times." A mature young man would say, "That is all fine and well my good friends. We will find other enjoyable things to do here at home" And so, I said, … "OK, you guys are a bunch of cowards and weenies, and I don't need you, and I'm just going to go camping all by myself!"

Well, I'll tell ya, this wasn't as dumb and emotional as it sounds. I did want to go camping, but not all alone. However, if I couldn't go off and do a brave thing, at least I could put on a show like I was brave enough to go off and do a brave thing. But no fool was I. I knew darn well that no rational adult is going to take an eight-year-old boy out deep into the woods and just leave him there all alone! Are they?

So, I played my role well. I put together all my gear. I got the food I would need to overnight in the wilds. I gathered some adventure gear: flashlight, knife, BB gun. I even got what I needed to take our two dogs with me, for protection, and loaded everything in the car.

I announced that I was ready to go.

OK!

Now is the time to explain to the kid why he can't go!

Now is the time to put the parental foot down and say, "NO!!"

I had made a fatal mistake. I had thought that my parents actually cared if something terrible happened to me. I was in error. This state of affairs was confirmed some years later when I overheard a conversation between my parents and my uncle, wherein they came right out and said that my brother and I were never wanted or loved by them. But that is a different story. For now, and on other occasions, this worked to my advantage. My brother and I got to go on many adventures that caring parents would have prevented.

So, off my father and I went.

I had thoughts that he just wanted a drive and would back out on the deal as soon as we got there.

But no.

As soon as I unloaded my stuff in the empty campground, my father hopped back in the car and was gone in a cloud of dust raised by the station wagon on the dirt access road.

Alone in the Woods

I chose a site, set up my crude camp, gathered firewood, and then, with my two dogs on leashes, set about adventuring. I caught a few frogs in a small stagnant-smelling pond, chased a squirrel up a tree, and caught a blue belly lizard.

Have you ever caught a blue belly? They are just lovely, gentle, little things. You turn them over and gently rub their little tummies that have these amazingly gorgeous blue sides, and it convinces them you are not a threat. They will then stand around on your shoulder for up to an hour or more, just seeming to enjoy your company and the higher view.

Anyway, I hiked around a bit, visited two old mines we had found before, and discovered a new one. But all too soon, the sky started to color, and it was time to head back to camp.

Even before I returned to the campground the smell of campfire smoke let me know that I was no longer alone in the woods. This came as a small relief to me, until I followed the wash around the bend and saw who my new companions were.

It was a small gathering of Hell's Angels!

There was no guesswork involved, any kid of those times would recognize their "colors" worn proudly on the backs of their leather vests. There were two bikes and an old van, four guys all together. Two were sitting on the top of the picnic table, one was by the fire, and the fourth fooling with one of the bikes. They hadn't seen me, so I stepped back behind a bush. I had heard plenty of stories about Hell's Angels. They were "bad news," criminals, wild outlaws. They would "just as soon kill ya as look at ya!!" Everybody knew that! Whatever was I to do? Should I turn around and go back into the hills? Should I sneak around them and run to the road and try to get help? But there was nobody around for miles. I couldn't just hide in the woods, it was getting dark, and I was getting hungry. As they were between me and my camp site, I had little choice but to try to quietly get past them and hope that they didn't notice me all evening. I could take care of myself, and besides, I had my two killer dogs with me.

OK, the dogs. Alright, my killer, protection dogs were, uh, so they were a Chihuahua-water spaniel mix, a bit bigger than a large house cat, OK! Not much help unless you were trying to catch a tame rabbit or a chicken without causing them harm, which they were pretty good at, but that was of no use to me here.

I could see that these fearsome guys had just come here to party, or hang out, for they had no camping stuff, just some beer and minor munchies. I headed for my camp. Stealthily, I made my way along the wash across the dirt parking lot from the campsites, trying to avoid detection, preparing myself for whatever action I may need to take. Then, they spotted me! @#%**#! The man tending the fire stood up! Uh oh! And then, it happened. They all smiled in a very friendly way and waved and then went back to what they were doing. I've got to say, I wasn't prepared for that.

Back in my space, I went about doing camp things. I got my fire lit, found a nice flat spot not too far from the table and fire ring for my sleeping bag, and set out my camp feast consisting of hot dogs, with a coat-hanger to cook them on, buns, some corn chips and cookies, and some marshmallows for later. You know, camp food.

Once I'd gotten things going and had a couple of hot dogs in me, the man who had been by the fire came over, beer in hand, with another of my neighbors. They were just as friendly as could be.

I politely offered some hot dogs and they politely refused saying that they had already eaten before coming out there. They were curious as to the whereabouts of the rest of my group. When I told them that I was alone they both seemed genuinely concerned. I told them that I was fine, that I had camped there a few times before, (leaving out that it had been with other people). It took a bit to convince them, but once I had they started calling me "Little Mountain Guy."

They stayed a while longer and we talked about the history and the mines and the gold, and about camping in nature and the freedom of the road. It made for a pleasant evening, and to be honest, I appreciated the company. Soon, however, they returned to their friends, and I went about cooking my marshmallows, taking care of and playing with the dogs, and making preparations for sleeping.

Just before I was to get into my old cloth sleeping bag, the fellas came back over to say goodbye, and to make sure that I really was OK. Then, with a goodbye wave, a cloud of dust, and the roar of Harley engines, they were gone. I listened to the sound of their bikes for a long time as their roar became a whisper and then faded into the distance. Then, there was only the sound of the wind. I was truly alone.

Perhaps here is where I should mention my lifelong phobia of being outdoors in the dark! It is only a phobia. My father, a PhD in psychology, explained how it is an irrational fear with no basis in reality. I understood and tried, because of my love of the night and the outdoors, to overcome it. But I sure felt it, then, and even now. I now live in the mountains and when I go out into the dark, almost every night, I still feel it. It's like a pebble in your shoe, you feel it, but it doesn't stop you from doing what you need to or want to do.

So, with fearful feelings crawling around inside me, I got into my bag on the ground, (I had no tent), gathered a small dog on either side of me, and settled down for what I hoped would be a long, peaceful rest until morning.

Peace was not to be had that night.

Sometime later, I was awakened by a sound. It was barking, coming from the woods. I looked around in the dim light of the moon, just cresting above the hill, and noticed the lack of small dogs. My steadfast guardians were not steadfastly guarding!

I arose, found my flashlight, and headed into the woods toward the ruckus. After a while, I found the wee beasties tormenting the spot where they must have seen a mouse duck into a hole in an old stump. I gathered the hounds and returned to camp. Learning from my mistake, I put them on their leashes and tied the leash ends together. Putting them once more on either side of me with the knotted leashes above my head, I regained the comfort of my sleeping bag. After a while I drifted off to sleep again.

Again, I was awakened. The waning moon was nearly half up in the sky so some time must have passed. The dogs were again missing!

Arising once more, I found my flashlight and entered the woods. (Let's not forget that phobia.)

Following the barks of frustration and disapproval, I found the miniature escape artists with their tethers, still tied together, wrapped around a small sapling. I disentangled the fugitives and, again, returned to camp.

Now, I may be a slow learner, but I can learn.

This time I put the dogs on either side first, then entered my bag and lay upon the leashes. That way, the dogs could not possibly leave without waking me. I could now go soundly to sleep, secure in the knowledge that small, defenseless animals of the woods would no longer be threatened by my larger, toothier ones that night. And so, sleep I did.

My eyes opened.

The moon was nearly fully up in the sky. There was a lightening in the eastern sky, announcing the coming dawn and putting some of the younger stars to sleep. The light dew that precedes the morning had fallen across the top of my sleeping bag razing a damp, slightly musty but not unpleasant, canvas smell.

But why was I awake?

Full consciousness comes slowly to a weary eight-year-old. And weary I was after a night of rude awakenings. I just lay still as I gained awareness of my surroundings. I heard a whimpering sound. This time the dogs were still with me, but they were both back behind my head. I tilted my eyes up and saw the once fearless dogs cowering and shivering. Their fearful gaze was over my head and toward the end of my sleeping bag. Then ….

Something stepped on my foot!

There are times in life when something very old within us, something primal, takes over. Something from a time when we, our species, cowered in the darkness, no houses, no tools, with only our meager wits and heightened awareness to keep us from becoming a meal for some larger, fiercer predator. This was one of those times for me.

I froze!

I didn't jump. I didn't suddenly look.

I very slowly tilted my gaze toward the sensation of pressure.

There, on the foot of my sleeping bag, standing in a crouched position ready to pounce, was a mountain lion!!

The big cat's eyes were narrowed and focused on what it must have thought was easy prey. The little dogs!

When it finally noticed me, its eyes widened in surprise for just a moment. In that instant, my adrenalin-fueled heightened awareness allowed me to clearly see, in the light of the moon and the coming dawn, the round, black pupils set in the pale eyes of the looming predator, and its upper lip drawn back in a strange grimace, exposing its huge white canines!

The cat's eyes narrowed again. This time, the focus was on me!

Author's backyard photo of a mountain lion with a fresh kill

Time seemed to slow down. My mind raced. What should I do?! What CAN I do?! I had a knife, but it was over on the table, too far away. (A mistake I would never make again.) I had a BB gun that might frighten it, but that was with the knife. I thought to myself, what do I know about lions? Who have I heard of that has ever been in this situation? And then it came to me.

Bugs Bunny!!

Yeah, Bugs Bunny the cartoon rabbit. It has been more than fifty years, so I no longer remember the story or the context, but, in one of his cartoons he was faced with a ferocious lion bent on having a rabbit snack. I do remember that Bugs calmly said, "Eh, I hoid somewheres that if you make a sudden loud noise, it will frighten away wild animals." With that, Bugs stretched up, arms waving over his head, and hollered something like, "YA LALALALALALA!!" The lion responded by rearing back up on his hind legs spinning and running off yelling, "IEE IEE IEE IEE," like a wounded dog!

Well …

It wasn't much, but it was all that I had to go on. I was dead out of options, and, if this didn't work, I would be just plain dead! Cat food!! So, I trusted my life to the words of a sarcastic, bumbling bunny.

Putting art into action, I sat up suddenly, waved my arms wildly over my head and hollered at the top of my lungs "YA LALALALALALAAA!!"

Well, I'll tell you the truth, that bunny is no liar.

That big kitty reeled up on its hind legs with eyes as big as the moon, spun around, and lit out for the hills just as fast as ever it could! I could almost hear it saying, "IEE IEE IEE IEE!" as it sped off into the distance.

Well, there you have it.

Bugs Bunny had saved my life. Not to mention the lives of two small dogs.

And my parents had said that I was wasting my time watching cartoons. Ha! Anyway, there would be no more sleeping that night.

The rest of my stay at Placerita Canyon was fairly routine. There was plenty to keep me busy until I was picked up at 5:30 that evening.

While all alone on that one trip, I had overcome a false fear and faced, head on, a real one. I had also caught three lizards, followed a rattlesnake across a hillside, discovered and explored three new gold mines, engaged and won the respect of a group of Hell's Angels, and fought off a mountain lion with nothing but my bare hands.

Like I said, a place of fun, history, and real adventure!

Day of the Dogs

This is a true story that has stayed vividly in my mind till this day. When I was a young person between the ages of four and twelve, I lived on a rural acre in the San Fernando Valley on a dirt road in Northridge, California.

I believe the layout of the property may have had something to do with the "day of the dogs." But of course, the landscaping alone can't explain this one-time phenomenon. The acre was fenced. The back, or north, portion was an orange grove with more than seventy-five orange trees. The house was in the center of the property with scores of various fruit trees on the west side and front, including some large landscaping trees.

The long driveway along the east side was lined from the gate to the back of the house with a boxwood hedge about two feet tall on either side. It is this feature to which I attribute some connection to the dog activity as once someone or some animal entered the gate, it was conducted directly to the hub of home activity. This, on many occasions, led many animals to come into my life, from monkeys to Brahma bulls to even a black panther on one occasion that had escaped from a circus that visited the fairgrounds at the end of our block.

Tending the hedges—one of my many chores

I had been born an unwanted child. I grew up with cycles of abuse and neglect, such that leads to a type of loneliness and longing that few who have experienced it can understand.

Perhaps these feelings were particularly acute on this day, but for reasons I could not explain then or now, I was visited by a succession of dogs. It was a summer day when I was eight, so I was home the whole day and the dogs would come all day long. Sometimes one dog, sometimes two dogs, sometimes even three at a time. They came in all breeds. From Basset Hounds to German Shepherds, from Chihuahuas to large dogs whose breed I could not identify, the dogs would come and in friendly fashion greet me. They would sit down and stay with me for a short time, very politely, like a visiting aunt.

They did not come for food, although some of them partook of the water I had available for them, once I realized this was a day of visitations. They seemed merely to come for the sole purpose of making a social call on me. And they would politely bid me adieu and head back down the long driveway.

In all twenty-eight dogs visited me that day! Almost all of them never to be seen by me again.

I always had an affinity for animals and as is common in the very young, felt an innate ability to communicate with them on their level. This all made for a delightfully (and abnormally for me) pleasant day. And as the twilight fell and the last of my canine visitors departed, I felt satisfied that this had been a good day. There has never been one like it before or since.

Conversing with Crows

When I was a young fellow, around eight or nine, I lived on a rural acre in the San Fernando Valley. The entire yard was filled with trees, most of which were the population of an orange grove.

On the back side of the property, the neighbors on either side had very tall eucalyptus trees, which, particularly to a diminutive young man, made an imposing wall across the sky. These trees also served to attract birds of many different species.

On this particular day around the onset of fall, just before school started, I was alone and at loose ends in the back yard. I noted what appeared to be a crow—or possibly a raven, as I had not learned to differentiate between the two at that age—in one of the eucalyptus trees closest to our yard.

I took it upon myself to strike up a conversation. As I was a child, and my voice was not yet locked in to one particular tonal range by adulthood, I had the ability, as many young do, to be quite a mimic. I chose a stealthy approach by hiding in one of the three small outbuildings that existed in the backyard.

These were: the "horse house," which apparently accommodated its namesake before our family moved to the property; the "door house," which was a conglomeration of various, and what I would now know as interesting antique doors, taken out of our house when it was remodeled and all nailed together in the form of a shed; and what we called the "Tiki house," which was little more than a framework with a roof, and that was surrounded by bamboo matting and thus relatively open to the environment, yet enough to conceal my form. And thus, I chose that structure to hide in.

I started by making a few cawing calls, which, to my surprise and delight, received an answer. When I would call, my avian companion would answer. I'm not sure what I said, but it seemed to strike a fervent note with my co-communicator. Our discourse soon attracted another of his kind. And then there were two.

Intrigued, I continued my calling and they continued theirs. And that attracted yet another and another. As I called from my hiding place, their numbers grew and their calls became louder, which in turn attracted even more.

It was not long before there were scores, perhaps hundreds, of the large black birds all calling at the tops of their lungs and filling the trees all around the yard. They were everywhere, raising quite a cacophonous clatter that continued, to my amusement, until I chose to step forth out of my concealment, and bid them salutations in person. To which all fell silent.

After a very short quiet spell, they began calling among themselves again. And the feathery, black crowd dissipated until I found myself once more alone.

I cannot be sure what I said to the beaky beasts that created such an uproar, but my guess is that somehow, I had hit upon a distress call that they took to be from one of their own. Perhaps one of their young. And the crowd was gathered to administer aid and support for that perceived unfortunate. However, most likely I will never know.

The Lighthouse Mother

When I was a child of about five, and basically an unwanted child, it was a natural response to seek the fulfillment of my need for maternal love and support from outside the family. As it happened, our elderly neighbor on that rural acre in the San Fernando Valley was at least for a short time, up to the task.

Paula Alexius was a kindly Estonian woman who, although she immigrated to the United States in the early part of the 20th Century, had a thick Estonian accent and a gentile European manner. For several months during the summer of my fifth year, my older brother and I would sneak over to the Alexius's almost every morning for pancakes and other goodies. If there is any gentleness in my nature, I can perhaps attribute that to Paula and George Alexius.

George passed away shortly after that in his mid-'80s, leaving Paula alone. Our family returned her kindness by watching over her in her later years, until, as she became more frail and had a few falling incidents, it was determined by her doctors that it was time for her to move into an old-age facility.

As she apparently had no family to inherit her personnel treasures, she told us to go into her house and take whatever we wanted so that it would not just go to the state. It was on doing so that I began to learn the true story of my kindly old neighbor's past.

Thinking back, to me it was a house filled with wonders, such that, even to this day, I wish that I could have rescued more of them. As I was still a child, and my parents had no sense of taste about these things, (they would take beautiful old antiques in good condition and sand them and paint them blue and green to make them "better" and "more modern"), I could only grab what I alone could carry. This amounted to an old crank record player; a record cabinet filled with old graphite records, some so old they only had recordings on one side; a couple old cameras; and what proved to be the most intriguing of the treasures, a very old leather suitcase filled with photographs and a few letters written in Estonian.

From studying these photographs, a romantic story of Paula's intriguing life began to emerge. Paula was born in Estonia in 1896 and there grew to be a lovely young woman, a Countess by some accounts. She married a Baron and would have lived a different extraordinary life there perhaps, if not for the rumblings of war and the specter of the Russian revolution. The two young nobles made a wise and fateful decision to immigrate to the United States.

I can only speculate as to why they chose to move to Alaska and become lighthouse keepers. Perhaps they found it difficult to assimilate or perhaps they just longed for adventure in the far northwest or were encouraged by friends already there to "come on out." But their fortunes led them to what must have, at that time, been one of the loneliest wilderness outposts in the world.

The Baron, August Von Waldenberg, was a diminutive man with a powerful bearing. Though half-a-head shorter than Paula—not a tall woman herself—he was a fine figure of a man. He carried out his duties as first assistant lighthouse keeper well, and soon worked his way to head lighthouse keeper maintaining the guiding lights at such far flung locations as Tree Point Lighthouse station, Guard Island LHS, and perhaps Eldred Island LHS and the storied Cape Spencer LHS.

It must have been a lonely existence for Paula and August with very few human contacts other than immediate lighthouse staff. And one can only imagine the solitude of the long Alaskan winters. Although the official housing was comfortable, and had many modern amenities, there were no social gatherings, no TV, and probably no radio other than for short wave communication.

It was at this time, in the early to mid-1930s, that August and Paula must have somehow run into George Alexius, or perhaps he was the friend that encouraged them to come there. But George is the man who would become Paula's second husband. George Alexius was a tall and dashing figure. He had been a highly decorated military officer, one of Teddy Roosevelt's Rough Riders and he too had been drawn to the wild and beautiful Alaskan fjords and the light house service at least as early as 1917.

They must have formed a rare and special friendship for the pictures evidence long distance visits and perhaps fond communication. There is one particularly intriguing set of photos showing, apparently upon all of their retirements in 1940, first August sitting next to his friend, George, along with another retiring lighthouse keeper, Sam Ellison. And then, almost the same photo with Paula, replacing August, sitting in the middle next to her future husband George.

My romantic heart speculates wildly at the possibilities of that three-way connection. Did George spend lonely Alaskan nights in a remote lighthouse longing for his forbidden secret love? Was Paula aware of George's secret? Did she share his feelings even then? Did August get inklings here and there of something intangible between his wife and his friend? Or was it simply that August, on his deathbed, charged his friend George to please take care of Paula for him? We will never know.

But what we do know, is that after retirement, George moved to Northridge in the San Fernando Valley to a one-acre corner lot between two dirt roads. The house had been built in the late 1920s or early 1930s when movies were just taking off a bit south in Hollywood.

The property seemed laid out to meet a movie star's needs, surrounded by tall trees and ivy-covered fences, creating a lovely private space around the house. There was a long barn that had various sections to it in a line. (In my time, the segments were in varying states of decay from pristine near the house, to nothing but a foundation and some posts at the extreme end.) And in the middle of the back yard, a row of five long, concrete shallow ponds for raising frogs for frog's legs. (Which in my time still held water after a rain and attracted frogs that provided all of our pollywog needs as children.)

Upon August's passing in 1948, Paula soon joined George on what they called their "Home Ranch," and were married. One can tell by the pictures from the following years that George and Paula seemed to make up for all their lonely years, isolated in lighthouses, in a faraway cold place. Their numerous pictures of tremendous outdoor parties showed lines and lines of tables laden with food and flowers, attended to by scores of smiling happy friends.

The obviously happy couple always seemed to be at the center of joyous social activities which continued right up until George's regrettable, but predictable, death.

Even I, child that I was, got to partake in some of the revelries next door. I even won my first can of house paint for twenty-five cents at a raffle at one of their parties. I did not know what I was going to do with it, but I was awfully proud to have won it.

I've often thought of Paula and George and of the Baron over the years. I still own most of the treasures that I carried from their happy Home Ranch on that sad occasion. My greatest treasures are my memories of, and even the questions about, these remarkable people. My only longing regret about their association with my life is that when I knew them well enough to feel parental love from them, I was not old enough or wise enough to ask a few more questions.

George and Paula at their Home Ranch

A Whale of an Adventure

They say it's the little things in life that count, but sometimes it's the big things.

I have had a … complicated … relationship with the sea. I have enjoyed its nature, its beauty, its extreme calm, and its serenity. On other occasions, it has tried to kill me!

To illustrate, please permit me to make a lot of "I have" statements to briefly enumerate a few of my more notable experiences with the sea. I have swum freely above the ocean depths more than a hundred miles from any land. I swam, with no more protection than bathing trunks, a mask, and a snorkel, with no less than a dozen hungry sharks, during a feeding frenzy. I have twice nearly been pulled down into Davy Jone's locker by a powerful maelstrom, once alone in the water and once in a small motorboat. As a merchant marine, my ship's only anchor was lost to a massive storm on my night watch, leaving all aboard at the scant mercy of an angry sea, twice.

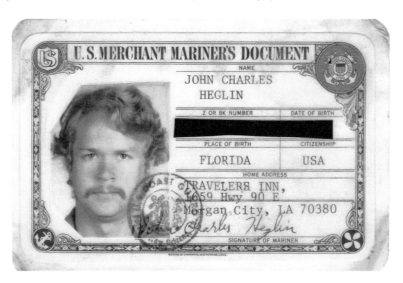

The helm was suddenly lost while at full throttle in busy shipping lanes, while I stood at the wheel. After being Shanghaied, I leaped from one ship to another at night, in rough seas.

On another occasion, my brother Jim and I jumped ship at risk of being hanged. I was bit by shark, faced a great white while in the water, suffered a giant stingray bite, and I have helmed many crafts through the sea, from an inflatable raft to a nuclear aircraft carrier. Each of these true-life experiences have a tale of their own, but for now, let me share a few memories from my youth that helped lead me to my various affairs and adventures with the sea.

Although my childhood was far from ideal, I did have some fortunate opportunities for interesting and unusual experiences. Some of these opportunities came through the mild rivalry between my father, who was a PhD, and my uncle JD, his older brother, who was a doctor, a GP, with his own practice. Both had raised themselves out of near poverty through hard work, education, and the GI Bill. Each, in his own way, wanted to show that they had "made it" in life. One of the ways Uncle JD demonstrated this affluence was that he had a sailboat.

OK, he actually had a piece of a boat.

OK, it wasn't really a "piece" of a boat, it was the whole boat but only for a piece of the time. You see, he and seven or ten other doctors went in on a sailboat together and each got to use the boat for a certain amount of time every couple of months throughout the year. It was a sleek two master, a "yawl" in nautical terms, meaningfully named by the group of docs the "Panacea."

Now, you need to know that these two boys were from Iowa. Iowa is not a state known for its famous sailors. However, if you are now living in southern California and want to run with the cool kids, having a sailboat is the way to go. And besides, they have books about sailing, don't they, and these two were proven at studying. What could go wrong?

One saving grace of the Panacea was it also had a motor. Therefore, we were spared the spectacle of watching the two, slightly inebriated, brothers try to enter and exit the dock and the port under power of sail only.

So, it was out to sea, and adventure was just over the horizon. Well, at least in the general direction of the horizon anyway. We never went any farther than the Channel Islands. Mostly over to Catalina and back. That was roughly twenty-one miles from wherever the last user of the boat had left it, so not exactly an around the world tour. However, we really were upon the high sea in a small boat and it was exciting and adventurous enough for all of us, and I, myself, have fond memories of the sights and smells and sounds that enveloped us.

The adventures came in all sizes. Some were big, like the time, while visiting Anacapa Island, Uncle JD put the Panacea's sheets to the wind, (while probably three sheets to the wind himself) and attempted to take us to Santa Barbara Island to the northwest. As we approached the north end of the island, the sea began to get rougher. Most of the two families retreated below into the cabin, a move I could never understand as doing so would just make me feel seasick. I needed, and enjoyed, the open space and fresh air, and so stayed up top and clung to the forward mast, the mainmast with Cousin Debbie, who was a year my senior. JD was at the tiller, just behind the mizzenmast, and my brother Jim was playing the bored teenager role, laying in his sleeping bag on the cushioned seats in the pit between the tiller and the cabin door, reading a comic book and ignoring the world.

As we emerged from the lee of the sheltering island, the wind, angry at being crammed between Anacapa and Santa Barbara, whipped the compliant ocean up into cresting, twenty-foot swells, far too much for the little boat that thought it could. The Panacea heaved and rolled with the sudden and persistent side seas, at one point leaving Debbie and I blasted with spray and hanging straight out from the mainmast like a couple of yardarms. Uncle JD, realizing his near-fatal mistake, swung us around back toward the relative safety of the island's lee. We made it back, (obviously, since I am telling you this story) but not before the brave little craft was completely swamped by a huge wave!

As we turned into the wind, the waves came at us head-on. A bad bump from behind tilted us nose down just as a particularly large wave hit us from the front. The bow plunged into it like a knife. As the swirling green sea crashed up over the deck, Debbie and I pulled ourselves up the mainmast onto the boom to avoid being swept off the boat. For just a moment, it seemed as though the entire hull of the boat was under water. I'll never forget looking back and seeing Uncle JD standing with the tiller in one hand a rope in the other, up to his waist in frothing water, with a look of fierce concentration on his face.

The little boat bobbed back up like a cork, and as the flood began to ebb, I realized that I'd lost sight of Jim. In the place where I last saw him there was naught but water, but as that water receded, I first observed the top of a comic book, then the hands holding it, the top of a head, then a face, a form, and as the last of the salty brine ran out of the scuppers, the whole of the ultimate bored adolescent, in a soggy sleeping bag, still staring at the graphic novel as though nothing had happened interesting enough to warrant his attention.

Not all of the adventures were filled with such drama. Many were more along the lines of pleasant, mundane adventures. Or should I say, mundane activities achieved in a novel and adventurous way.

Like going to the movies. In Avalon, on Catalina, there is a huge, beautiful old casino out by itself on a point of land on the northern curve of the harbor. Within is included a large ballroom dance floor, and in the lower part of the massive circular building is, or at least was, a marvelous old-style movie theater.

Now it just so happened that on one of the occasions that the Panacea lay anchored in Avalon Harbor, "The Magnificent Seven" was playing in the casino theater. For many of us kids this was a must-see event. Seeing as the parents had already planned on some important drinking on board that evening and had already engaged in that effort to some extent, there was little difficulty in obtaining permission to abandon ship. So, five little kid-lings (the oldest of us being perhaps eleven), set out to sea in a tiny little six-foot dingy appropriately christened the "Panic."

All that we had to do was get from the boat to the dock at the casino. It was only about a quarter of a mile, but we had to navigate through all of the other boats and ships at anchor in the harbor. We tried various rowing positions with the five of us, finally settling on one in the front, two in the back, and the two in the middle side by side each operating one oar. We tried various combinations pulling at the oars. Younger cousins Mike and Jon Jon—called that to distinguish him from myself as I was the older John—we barely moved in any direction, and everyone got splashed. Cousin Debbie and Mike—we just went in circles. Finally settling on brother Jim and myself and we had positive motion. With Debbie in front calling direction and the boys in the back staying out of the way, we made headway toward the casino and didn't even run into any other boats or anchor lines.

It was a lovely transit. The fresh smell of the salt air mixing with dozens of strange and exotic odors, the sound of the oars rhythmically plunging in and out of the water combined with the lapping of the wavelets against the hull of the little craft, along with the thwacking of the port-slacked rigging against the masts on the various other boats in the harbor as they gently rocked and pulled at their moorings, made us feel like true sailors of old. The casino made a gorgeous beacon for us to follow as it towered over the rainbow-flecked water like an enormous round castle, illuminated by the light reflected from the orange and gold and cotton candy-pink clouds catching the last rays of the sun as it set behind the silhouetted island.

Once we had made our way across the harbor and tied the Panic up along with several other launches at the tiny dingy dock, we made our way to the theater. The theater was cavernous, with row upon row of large comfortable red velvet seats that flipped up for easier passage. The walls sort of curved up into the ceiling, dome-like, with stars painted on the top and elaborate murals painted around the edges. The movie screen was nestled beneath a giant double proscenium arch, and above the center, with elaborate abstract designs flowing down from either side, was a rendering of Botticelli's "The Birth of Venus" standing on her clamshell in all her naked glory.

Seeing as we got there early and had the whole of the theater's seating to choose from, we chose what we considered the best seats in the house, the center of the front row.

What a great time we had drinking sodas and munching popcorn and milk duds while watching that magnificent movie. Watching those bad guys trying to be good guys, fighting bad guys who were much "badder" bad guys than our good bad guys. Watching Yul Brynner and Steve McQueen, twenty-feet tall, fighting the good fight against insurmountable odds, and above all, the action, seeming to glow out of the ceiling, a beautiful naked Venus smiling down at me. What more could a prepubescent young fella ask for?

We all left the theater chattering like magpies, going over our favorite scenes from the movie, shooting each other and dying repeatedly as we wandered the halls of the casino and then down the path to the dock. We kept up the lighthearted repartee as we boarded the little dingy, untied her, and pushed out into the harbor. Then we fell silent all at once. Just where had we left the Panacea? It was light out when we rowed over, and we barely made it there with a monolith of a building to guide us. Now it was quite dark, and the Panacea was one boat among eighty or ninety others, row upon row in the darkness. We had ourselves a bit of a quandary, and we couldn't even hope for any help from the parents seeing as we had the only means for them of leaving the boat with us. It looked like the crew of the "Panic" was about to panic!

However, cooler heads prevailed, and I suggested a systematic search. All boats were south of the casino and us. I figured we had come past several boats on the way in so should start the search at least three rows in. The Panacea was not near the outside edges of the moorage so there was no need to look there.

With those parameters in mind, we set off on our search. What had been scenic and charming in the daylight took on a whole new, weird, and creepy aspect in the dark.

Back and forth we went, from east to west and back again, looking hopefully at each rocking white hull until it proved a stranger to us, and we lurched onward toward the next rolling hulk. We moved on in almost silence as the fearsome spirit of the sea had a grip on us. We imagined horrible creatures and sea monsters writhing in the sinister black waters all around and under us, and weren't we riding awfully low in the water with five people in this tiny dingy? Even the boats we approached appeared as krakens, towering over us, tottering to and fro. And our fears were not entirely unfounded. Many awful things have happened in these waters. Including, a few years later, the body of the lovely actress Natalie Wood was found floating near the bottom in just this spot, having mysteriously drowned on a dark night just like this.

It was after eleven by the time we dragged our damp, exhausted, little bodies up the side ladder and into the boat's cabin. The parents were pretty much right where we had left them, although, a little more subdued. I don't think that they had noticed that we were gone.

The long hours that we spent under sail to and from the islands were, for the most part, uneventful. Without much to do, we kids would entertain ourselves with simple things, such as sitting on the boom and just laying back into the belly of the mainsail, like a sort of vertical hammock, and just letting the rocking of the waves lull us to sleep.

Or, like sitting with our legs dangling over the bow, leaning on the small metal railing, watching the flowing water for whatever crossed our path. This included a lot of seaweed, jellyfish, rarely porpoises, but mostly sharks, (lots of sharks!) lurking menacingly just beneath the surface. Once, we counted 178 sharks in one hour!

And, sometimes, two or three of us would ride along in the Panic, which was always tethered to the stern by a long rope and followed the sailboat like an awkward puppy. This was a particular favorite pastime of mine. Grab some cans of soda, a few snacks and a few cushions, and just kick back and slide across the surface of the sea. We would let the tow rope all the way out and hang back about seventy-five feet or so from the Panacea, far enough as to not be able to hear any grumbling parents or squabbling siblings or cousins. It was like being adrift alone in the sea, with just sounds of the water rushing past, mixed with the occasional call from a sea bird, the smell of the salt spray and the feel of it on your face cooling the heat from the shining sun overhead, and always there was the gentle lift and drop of the waves. In a stressful world it was always quiet, relaxing, and peaceful.

That is, until it wasn't.

On one terrifying occasion, fate had something else in mind. It started out fairly normal. We were on the long haul from Catalina to Long Beach harbor, running with the wind in fairly calm seas. Debbie, Jim, and I decided to hang back in the dingy. We had been back there, with the tow rope at full length, for about fifteen minutes, just relaxing into the rhythm of the swells, when it seemed as though the sea next to us began to rise up, piling up upon itself, and with a roar of rushing water, a strange dorsal fin rose out of the water, about six feet off our port side. The fin was attached to the biggest back I'd ever seen on a fish. It was nearly twice the length of the Panic, and that was just the part sticking out of the water. It appeared to be that the biggest God damned shark anyone had ever seen was scoping us out for dinner!

There was panic on the Panic!

From a fish perspective, the Panacea was a trawler, and we were the bait at the end of the long line. A state of affairs that we, the bait, did not find acceptable at all. Immediate action was taken to rectify the situation. Jim, quite—shall we say—

heavy at that point in his life and somewhat lethargic in nature, suddenly transformed into a fast-motion-rope-pulling machine, creating quite a wake off the dinghy's bow as we shot forward toward the sailboat. Our new friend kept pace with us all the way to the stern of the mother ship where, upon arriving, dear brother Jim leaped aboard to safety, dropping the rope and sending us spinning backward with the force of his disembarkation.

Now, a funny thing happens when a small craft in the water suddenly loses its source of locomotion. Whether being pulled or pushed, it very quickly comes to a relative standstill. This we did after rotating nearly half a turn to port. However, the sailboat continued on its course at a fairly rapid pace, that seventy-five feet of slack line being taken up fast until it snapped taught like a bowstring, yanking and spinning us around with such force that we were thrown to the floor and the little dingy took on a substantial amount of water.

We floundered a bit amid the floating soda cans and potato chip bags in the bottom of the boat, wet, bruised and confused, but only for a moment because our massive-finned friend rose up again, and was once again right next to us. This, of course, spurred us back into action. Debbie, who was built like a small female version of Hoss Cartwright from the TV show *Bonanza*, and had a similar amiable disposition, took up the panicked position of hauling us in while I began to bail out the water that made us ride low and impeded our forward progress. Our personal sea monster stayed right alongside, and just as we reached the stern of the mother ship, the beast let out a tremendous roaring blast of air and water, startling Debbie so much that she instinctively jumped onto the Panacea, once more sending me spiraling to a potential appointment with Davy Jones.

For the second time, when I reached the end of my rope, I was violently wrenched back into motion, but this time I was ready for it. Furthermore, I was much calmer, for I had come to a realization, the horrible terror of the deep that had given us such a start, was not the man-eating, flesh-ripping monster shark that we had taken it for. Sharks don't have blowholes! It could only be a whale. And I realized that unless it had mistaken me for some guy with a wooden leg, a harpoon, and a bad attitude, I should be in little or no danger.

By now, the two ship-jumping rats that had abandoned me to a gruesome fate had, in barely coherent ramblings, informed the—to that point clueless—parents of the horrible fate that awaited us all. In good captain form, Uncle JD handed off the tiller, jumped back, and began hauling me in as fast as he could, a frantic look on his face. I continued bailing, but only halfheartedly, for, no longer fearful, I was watching this enormous sea mammal that had for some reason befriended us, with curious fascination. The huge, gray, slightly mottled back slid smoothly through the water alongside me with a rhythmic undulating motion. It seemed so graceful and effortless. If I looked down into the clear water I could see where the gray top color gave way to the light color of the underbelly, but I was too close to see the overall shape and size. I can only assume that the big critter could see me as well, for it once again followed the dingy up to the stern of the sailboat, but, once I jumped aboard, it stayed with the sailboat and never followed the dingy again.

From that point began a wonderful dance between us and the whale. The massive mammal seemed to find in us an object of some curious affection. Whether it was us or the boat itself that attracted the sensuous cetacean was hard to tell, but it was clear that something about us was very interesting to the friendly beast. It, and I say "it" because no one on board was qualified to determine the sex of the animal, would swim alongside for a spell, occasionally blowing great plumes of mist into the air. Then it would suddenly dive and go directly under the boat where it would roll over, showing us its great white belly through the clear water, and swim that way for quite some time before rolling topside up and surfacing on the other side of the boat with a great roar of mist. Some of the cousins hid down in the cabin, crying and cowering with fear, but to the rest of us it was a beautiful and fascinating display. Sometimes it would swim deeper in the blue and sometimes on the surface, but never very far away.

That is how it went for close to an hour, with our own private whale friend keeping pace, going back and forth under the boat while we would run back and forth on the deck from side-to-side marveling at such a wonder. Then, as quickly as it had arrived, our friend headed off in another direction. We watched as the last couple of mist blasts receded into the distance and then we were alone again, with only the rustling of the wind in the sails and the rolling calm of the sea.

The author on the short rope.

The Problem with Poaching Pumpkins

When I was but a young lad of perhaps ten years of age, I was involved in a walk on the metaphorical, "wild side." (Okay, more like a walk on the slightly naughty side.) At any rate, a departure from my normal M.O. of, "Try to be as good as you can and perhaps you won't be punished today." Admittedly a failed strategy in my case, but that is yet another story.

In my defense, I was provoked on this occasion beyond reason into my minor, almost, crime-wave by circumstances so insanely intolerable they practically demanded action on my part.

You see, pumpkins were going to waste!

That's right, you read correctly, PUMPKINS, those joyous wonderful happy harbingers of Halloween, were **going to waste!!**

Perhaps I should explain a bit. Halloween was my very favorite holiday. Hell, it was pretty much my favorite anything. This was for several reasons. I liked trick-or-treating. Sure, I liked the candy OK, but what I liked about it most was that you got to walk right up to every house in the neighborhood and they would open the door and you would get to look inside and kinda see how they lived. Cool! But the thing that most profoundly endeared me to Halloween was that on that night you could be anybody or anything you wanted, and I desperately wanted to be almost anybody else. My childhood was not a happy one. I am sure there were those who had worse, but mine was quite bad enough, thank you. Therefore, starting around August, I would become highly attuned to any reference to 'ween. My interest would be piqued by anything orange and black, any ghosts or skulls, and especially jack-o-lanterns, or just pumpkins.

My pumpkin friends

Well, anyway, I came upon this irksome knowledge when, while riding with my mother, we stopped at a local farm stand adjacent to a large field of primarily pumpkins. Seeing a large number of the orange orbs out there, and noting a lack of picking activity, I asked about their fate. The friendly farm fella informed me that it was the end of the season, and besides, most of the punkies were odd shapes or ugly and would be left to rot in the field and return to the soil.

Horrors!

I decided then and there that I had to **do** something about this sacrilegious squash squandering.

As soon as I arrived back home, I set about procuring a pumpkin posse. Though my cause was noble, I could only persuade one comrade to join my quest.

I will refer to him as BG. He may be a lawyer or a Senator now for all I know, and proof of purloining pumpkins in one's past could pulverize a political career.

Our plan was to take our bikes and try to arrive at the pumpkin patch just at dusk. It was a short ride in a car but a bit of a grunt on a bicycle, almost two miles, but I knew the way. I even knew a back way through neighborhoods so we didn't have to ride much on the busy streets.

The farm stand was at the bottom of what we kids called "You're Gonna Die Hill." This thing was aptly named, I can tell you from first-hand experience! Firstly, it was a relatively busy road, with cars whizzing by at around forty-five mph. There was no sidewalk and nothing like a bike lane in those days. The asphalt would have just run off into the dirt except it was on a hill, a steep hill, and running water from when it rained had eroded the dirt away so that it was a sharp two to four inch drop off the pavement onto deeper ruts and rocks. Now, here is the "You're Gonna Die" part. It was, as I said, a steep hill, a *very* steep hill. The steepest hill in my youthful experience. And most of us kids didn't have fancy, expensive bikes with fancy brakes and lots of gears. We had bikes with one gear, and you'd pedal if you wanted to move and stop pedaling if you wanted to stop. You would just slam all your weight back on the pedal on the upswing and lock up the rear tire. If the rear wheel was moving the pedals were moving. If you wanted to coast, you had to take your feet of the pedals which would keep on turning. Once you started down that hill, gravity would get a firm grasp on you and pull you down faster and faster, till your legs could no longer keep up the pace, and your feet would fly off the pedals and you would have to hold them up out of the way because the pedals were now whizzing around like an insane buzz saw. Now you had no way to control your speed at all. The hill would just continue to pull you down faster and faster, and your handlebars would start shaking, and your only hope was to maintain control and stay on the road until the hill leveled out at the bottom. However, by now you are going faster than the cars right next to you. If you choke and wipe out, your only choices are run off the road to the right and be mangled by the rocks and ruts before being thrown at high speed into a barbed wire fence, or be ground into hamburger on the pavement to the left before being run over by a car.

I only rode my bike down that hill twice. (Hey, I was a young, male idiot, do you think I could learn after only once?) And, I must add, just for the record, I did not die.

Our plan, thankfully, did not include riding down "You're Gonna Die Hill." The pumpkin patch covered the entire south face of the hill, from the farm stand at the bottom and butting up to a dirt road at the top. That dirt road across the top was our destination.

After making our excuses to our respective parents, we hopped on our bikes and headed out with nothing but one flashlight, my trusty camp knife, and two gunnysacks each.

Does anybody remember gunnysacks? When I was a kid all kinds of things came in them, from charcoal to potatoes to animal feed. They were always made of burlap and were strong and rough and easy to roll up and carry on the book rack of a banana seated stingray bike.

Well, we headed out east meandering through the neighborhood streets toward our target. It took a while longer than I had anticipated, but my aim was true, and we arrived at the top of the patch just as night was falling. The sun had set, and the lovely rose and violet Belt of Venus was slowly rising in the cloudless sky to the east following on the heels of a nearly full harvest moon.

Once we had ascertained that we were unobserved, we, literally, ditched our bikes and took up a surveillance position in the ditch between the road and the barbed wire fence overlooking the field. How did we come by all these skills? One of our favorite TV shows of the time was *Combat* with Vic Morrow before he got onto movies and, quite literally, lost his head making the *Twilight Zone* movie. At any rate, we had vast experience diving into ditches, crawling on our bellies and keeping a lookout from playing army over the years. And barbed wire fences? We were kids, we went through those like we were walking through air.

Looking down from our hilltop vantage point, we could see that the farm stand was closed for the night. We then moved through the fence and, keeping low even though we saw no people in sight, we moved down, out into the pumpkin patch like Snoopy in *It's the Great Pumpkin Charlie Brown*. The cool air was filled with the scent of slightly damp earth and pumpkin vines. Pumpkins of every shape and size were everywhere. The slightly spiky vines and leaves clawed at our clothes as we crawled from pumpkin to pumpkin cutting free the ones we found interesting with the camp knife and stuffing them into the gunnysacks.

Everything went smoothly as we crawled around the vine-covered hillside. Except, at one point, when a car pulled into the parking lot of the farm stand below us. We hit the dirt and froze as the headlights panned across the hillside. Our hearts pounded as we envisioned ourselves being arrested by the Pumpkin Police and taken down to Pumpkin Jail. However, it turned out to be just a car turning around to go back on the road.

At last, we poached one last pumpkin and hauled our sacks up to where our bikes lay in the ditch. Now all we had to do was hop on the bikes and ride home triumphant. But, there was a small flaw in our planning. How does one ride a bicycle carrying two large sacks of pumpkins, each of which can barely be lifted?? We tried every possible combination of positions we could think of. One sack held onto each handle grip. Too heavy to steer. One between the handlebars and one on the back. Too hard to control with one hand. One on the book rack, one on the lap. You ever try pedaling a bike while holding a heavy, lumpy sack with your knees?

At last, we gave up any hope of riding and resigned ourselves to walking home while pushing the bikes which would carry most of the weight. And so, off we set.

It was a long ride to get to the patch, but it was a very long walk to get home. Home is where we wanted to be, but wanting something does not make it so. The early evening of fall had fallen fully. It was now quite dark; the autumn moon had risen high and a slight chill in the air whispered to us that winter was soon planning to return after its long absence. Now, as we walked through the suburban neighborhoods, struggling to balance our gourd-engorged gunnysacks on our overburdened bicycles, we became painfully aware of the time.

The adventure had taken longer than we had anticipated. The hour was not late but it was something else, the dinner hour. The aromas of various foods being cooked throughout the neighborhood wafted through the air, clawing at our stomachs. We passed a house where fish was being fried, we slowed a bit. Another had hamburgers grilling in the backyard, we lingered. The next was cooking liver and onions, we practically ran past that one. And, at yet another, they were frying chicken, we nearly knocked on the door and asked if they would please adopt us!

By now the stress and strain of our endeavors was starting to take a toll. The excitement of our clandestine escapade had worn off and we were just plain tired from the exertion. Yet, we had a long way to go before we could rest, and BG began to worry about what punitive measures might be employed if our return was too tardy. The fatigue, and now hunger, seemed to increase with each step. Our purloined punk-patch prisoners seemed to always be trying to escape their burlap restraints. Every hundred steps or so we had to stop and readjust for balance, and we had maintained this drudging dance for the better part of a mile so far. The wisdom of our each carrying **two** sacks of contraband began to weigh on us, both figuratively and literally, and the exact personal value of the quantity of our questionably obtained cargo came into question.

I came to a decision, we needed to lighten our load.

But how exactly does one unload superfluous pumpkins? I hatched a plan. We would donate them to the needy! And after all, doesn't everybody need at least one pumpkin??

Now we needed to put my plan into action. Quickly, I might add, because we had to lighten our load and get moving if we were to avoid the punishment hour. You know, that hour between getting hollered at for being late, and, best not to go home at all, just change your name and move to another country.

So, taking one of my least loved pumpkin charges, (a very tough choice indeed) I chose a nice-looking house that lacked any punks on display. One that looked like the occupants would be willing to give a good home to an orphaned pumpkin in need. Then, with the raw nerve of a secret agent, and the cunning and reflexes of a cat burglar, I stealthily made my way to the front porch. Looking around to be sure I was unobserved, I strategically placed my potential pie package and ran like a squirrel with its tail on fire, retrieved my burlap burdened bike and we made tracks down the road, trying to appear as innocent as was possible for a pair of pre-adolescent pumpkin poachers. We watched over our shoulders and waited for the swat team with dogs and helicopters to descend upon us, but none came and so we were in the clear.

Like they say, it gets easier after the first one, so we would head down the road a bit, find a needy-looking house, pause for some quick action, and head off again one pumpkin short. In all, I suppose, we adopted out more than a dozen pumpkins to what we hoped were loving families. I can only imagine what people must have thought when they came out of their houses and were greeted by gregarious gourds. At any rate, once we had unloaded enough of our little orange friends, we could put the rest in one bag each, and hugging the bag on the front of the seat with one hand and steering with the other, we could finally ride our bikes again. In short order, we were safely back home, before the punishment hour and with only a minor hollering at for our tardiness.

We had observed a need, made a plan, and set out on an adventure. We had encountered some difficulties along the way, but what true adventure does not? We had lost some of our hard-won pumpkins, but we were not disappointed. The two of us had rescued a lot of pumpkins from rotting in the field, and hopefully, brought some pumpkin joy to several strangers. BG and I each managed to get home with more pumpkins than either one of us had ever had before, for the holiday season. He had eight and I ended up with nine. We had to be very selective in who we told about exactly how we came by such abundance. However, for a short time that year we were the envy of all who knew us.

And that was the only time that I ever strayed from the rules and mores of social convention. Well, that is, except for "The Great Pipe-sticker Robbery." But, of course, that is a completely different story!

Pumpkins from author's backyard.

Some Mammoth Undertakings

Whern I was just a young fella between the ages of about ten to fifteen, my Uncle Jack had a timeshare called "The Sierra Nevada Inn" up at Mammoth Lakes. A couple of times a year our family would join his family for a mountain adventure, sometimes in winter and sometimes in summer. Whenever we went, there was sure to be some kind of notable occurrence. To relate them all could fill a book, so I'll just start with a few of the standouts.

SCARE BEAR

On the occasion of a summer visit to the Mammoth Lakes region of the Sierra Nevada I had what might seem an unusual encounter with a rather large black bear.

My family had joined my uncle JD's family at their timeshare in that area. That day we were all visiting one of the beautiful lakes of the region, and we kids had been pestering the adults to rent us a motorboat to adventure around the lake in. The parents were in the bar of the lake lodge as was their custom, that being their favored recreational choice.

It was a fact known to us young folk that after the adults had been in the bar for a certain amount of time, they became more pliable, and we could often easily bend them to our collective will. It was our will this day to go out in a little motorboat.

It is almost impossible to get bored in such a place, with cousins, and all that nature, and trees and rocks to climb and the lake, but in our ramblings, we had observed others motoring around the lake and it looked like new fun to us. So, with a small amount of whining and wheedling, five of us were soon joyfully heading out into the heart of the alpine lake in a little boat, to find whatever adventure we could.

However, we never even had the chance to get into mischief! The lovely lake that had been a beautiful mix of glittering greens and blues covered with shimmering flecks of pure, liquid silver when we left the little dock, suddenly, within moments, became leaden and dull gray.

The lake begins to darken
("Hole in the Wall," in the background)

One of the things that I love about the Sierras is the unpredictability of the weather. It really keeps you on your toes. The temperature can swing as much as ninety degrees in a single day. I have climbed up a mountain in clear, sunny, eighty-five-degree weather, and climbed down in the snow … in June! The Sierras teach you to always be prepared, and that is a good lesson to be learned no matter where you are, or what you are doing.

Well, no sooner had we reached the center of the lake, than a massive thunderstorm materialized right over us. A group of grumpy clouds from the east, bent on seeing the west, had run smack into the peaks of the Sierras and were forced to stop and pay a water toll to cross over, which made them very angry, and they were going to let everyone know about it by throwing an electric tantrum!

Now, I love a good thunderstorm, but even we kids knew that if lightning is flying all over the place the last thing you want to be is the highest point in a lake. So, although disappointed, we turned around and sped as fast as we could back to the little dock, then ran into the lodge to escape the rain.

Our disappointment over our lost adventure was palpable, and now, we could tell from the loud crashing and smashing that was shaking the little lodge, we were missing one hell of a show outside! The only large windows faced out back, away from the storm-ravaged peaks. However, through those windows, we could see a row of wooden picnic tables with umbrellas, about thirty yards away that would have a perfect view of the action. So, the choice was to stay in the musty old lodge choking on cigarette smoke from the bar and miss all the excitement, or skip over to the tables, outdoors in the fresh air, with smells of the storm and the light rain on pine needles and loamy earth and observe one of nature's great wonders.

The four of us that bolted forth barely got damp on the run to the covered table with the best view.

What a dazzling electromagnetic display! Bolt after bolt slamming into the crags and trees surrounding the little glacier carved valley, lighting up the sky like an insane fireworks display. And the thunder, blasting and echoing all over like some war cannons from Hell, shaking the air and the ground and the table that we sat on. We just sat there, in silent awe, watching the amazing spectacle all around us.

At one point a bolt crashed somewhere behind us and, almost as a reflex, I looked back. I didn't see where it might have struck, but I did see, across the small clearing, in the woods about eighty feet behind us, something moving! Something big! I brought this to the attention of my table mates and all eyes turned to see.

It was a bear, a large bear, a black bear, although one with a dark brown coat! (Black bears come in all colors from jet black to light tan.)

The bear stopped at the edge of the forest and seemed to hesitate. It paced back and forth there, at the clearing's edge, all the while looking straight at us! There was a flash and another loud clap of thunder, and that seemed to make up the bear's mind. Without another moments' pause, it left the trees and charged straight at us, running full out!

Bears!

A bear of the author's acquaintance

If you look up the most dangerous mammals in North America, one of the first on the list is bears. With black bears, it is mostly because people do stupid things like try to get a picture of their kid riding on one of the bear's cubs or some other idiotic thing.

I grew up with bears, since I was about five years old. Before it was illegal to feed park bears, we used to make bear traps when we were little kids. No, not the big, toothy, leg crunching things they use in cartoons. Our traps consisted of a stack of tin cans with a sausage on top. The idea was, if a bear is in the area and finds the sausage, it will knock over the cans making a big clatter, alerting us to go out and see the big fuzzy beast.

I remember one occasion when I was about seven and we were staying in one of the small cabins at Giant Forest in Sequoia National Park, word went around the cabins that there was a bear in the vicinity. My brother Jim and I rushed out to set our trap. Once it was built, we ran behind the nearest cabin and peered around the corner to watch for the big bad bruin. So, there we were, the three of us looking around the corner, Jim on top, me in the middle, and the big brown fuzzy face on the bottom ... wait a minute! Big brown fuzzy face! Yeowee!! While we were intently watching our trap, the bear had come up behind us, and seeing two man-cubs enthralled by something around that corner, the curious beast joined in to see what the big deal was.

Another of the author's friends

We loved to see black bears! We were fascinated by them. I respect them and their ways, but I don't fear them. They, although potentially dangerous if mistreated, generally mean us no harm. They just want our stuff if they can get their big, grubby paws on it. I can honestly say that over my lifetime, being a mountain loving fella, I have had hundreds of encounters with bears, and never felt a threat.

So, a very large bear was charging right at us! One cousin took off in the opposite direction, toward the lodge, whining like a scared puppy. The rest of us, however, held our ground. Not so much because we were so brave, but because, by now, we could clearly see the critter's face. If you have ever known a dog, and seen that dog frightened by something, then you know the expression. This bear wasn't attacking anybody, it was just plain scared out of its wits. The poor critter had been terrified by all the lightning and thunder. It had seen the group of us under the umbrella, apparently not afraid, and decided that, even though we were young humans, being with us was far better than facing the storm alone.

As soon as the bear arrived at our table, there was an amazing moment of instant inter-species communication. Our new friend looked up at us with pleading eyes that clearly said, "Can I please stay here with you guys until this big scary noisy thing goes away?" And our answer, which we gave in human words, but more importantly in soothing, caring tones, was, "You can stay with us! Don't be afraid. It's all going to be OK." Even my brother, not known to be much of a softy, took pains to help calm the huge animal, and make it feel welcome to stay with us.

The storm rumbled on. We divided our time, and our interest, between the amazing spectacle of the huge storm, and the fascinating opportunity of spending time in very close proximity to a huge befuddled wild animal. There would be a bolt that would crawl across the sky with a flash, then a massive rumbling crash. We would give delighted exclamations of "WOW!" and "Dang!" Then one or more of us would turn back, look the bear in the eyes, and say calming things to the newly re-agitated beast.

By now, the "scared puppy" had made his way back to the lodge, and through it into the bar, and set about convincing the parents to come look out the window to watch while we were all being eaten by a big hairy monster. While wisely dubious of the whiner's tale, they nevertheless felt compelled to at least look. Upon doing so the scene that played out before them probably would have driven more caring, or sober, parents to some form of heroics, but in this strange case unnecessary, action. After all, here were three kids sitting within petting distance of a big-fanged, deadly-clawed wild-eyed bear that was so large that it easily outweighed all three kids put together. However, things being what they were, they called all the others in the bar over and just stood and stared, drinks in hand, without moving, so that, from our prospective, they looked like a wide-eyed, open-mouthed mural painted on the side of the lodge.

We only waved and smiled, and then went about watching the storm and calming our bear.

After a while, the lightning became less and less frequent, and the rain stopped. The sun began peeking through the clouds in glorious moving rays, spotlighting the lake and forest. Then, as quickly as it had begun, the storm was over. The sun shone brightly on the raindrops still clinging to the needles and leaves of the trees, turning them into a million prismatic diamonds, bedazzling all who beheld them. An aura of peace and calm fell over the little valley.

We turned to our big furry friend, and once more there was a moment of perfect inter-species communication. With an air of relief, the bear clearly said with its eyes and expression, "Thank you!" and then, turning with what I would swear was a smile on its face, that terrible, scary bear slowly walked straight into the woods, and was gone. We watched till we could no longer see the beast, and then, with no more bear, and no more storm, we left the shelter of our table and headed out to see what adventure we could find.

I guess if there is something to be learned it's this: we **cannot** let fear or prejudice rule our lives. We cannot let the fear of what might happen, or how we may fail, keep us from trying to live life to the fullest or from being open to new ideas. If we do, we may miss out on some of life's great experiences. To live in this fearless way is also almost a definition of innocent youth.

And so, on that day, there we sat, three young humans on the old wooden table, with our feet on a bench, facing the storm, and one large, frightened black bear, standing with its damp, shaggy side up against the table top (there was no bench on that side) sharing a big umbrella and an understanding that when things get scary, we all need each other to get through!

THE ICE BOY COMETH

As I recall, I must have been eleven going on twelve when, during a winter visit to the Twin Lakes area of Mammoth, my father, my brother, and I, leaving my uncle and a cousin or two at the lodge, took off with our sled heading south in search of the perfect hill.

The area around the lakes wasn't nearly as built-up as it is now, and the lodge was pretty much the only thing accessible and open near the lakes that winter, so our walk down the east side of the lake was wintry and beautiful and very isolated. The snow was not new so not much of it still clung to trees, but it was still soft and fresh-looking on the ground and the surrounding mountain peaks. The awesome beauty was almost overwhelming as was the hushed silence of the frozen forest. The three of us forged on with uncharacteristic reverence, speaking hardly a word.

Sled in tow, we followed a snow-covered road, which had only a few ski tracks and footprints, at least a quarter of a mile, until we came to a bridge (drive-able in summer) across to the other side of the lakes. Standing at the midpoint of the bridge, we looked out across the broad white expanse that was the lake. Frozen over completely, it looked very much like a meadow that was perfectly flat, except where it sloped up slightly where it met the undulating shoreline.

Our excursion to the far side of the lake was no more fruitful in our search for the perfect sledding hill, but it made little difference. The snow was too soft and deep for the type of sled I had, it being a Flexible Flyer-style with narrow steel runners more suited to hard packed snow or ice. So, I had given up the quest, very content to just wander and explore, the sled following behind like a loyal dog.

It was just as beautiful and interesting on this side of the lake and we soon spread out in different directions, each being attracted by a different object or feature. I headed north a few hundred yards along the shore toward an intriguing shape in the snow: A strange, lifted circle. Was it an ancient ritual site? Was it an object proving alien visitation? It turned out to be nothing more than a campground fire ring.

Starting to feel a bit chilled in the fifteen-degree weather, in spite of my thermal underwear, coat, and gloves, I began to think of heading back. I looked around for the others. To my surprise, I saw them already on the other side of the lake! They, too, had decided to head back. They just hadn't bothered to inform me!

I shouldn't have been surprised. It wasn't the first time my family had left me behind for the polar bears. It was just the first time it had been so almost literal!

Now at this point I had two choices. I could head back to the bridge, go all the way around and never catch up to them. or …

OK, I know what you are thinking. I'd have to be crazy to try to cross the lake.

Well, I'm not as dumb as I look! (I'm told that would be practically impossible!) Remember, it was the dead of winter. It was fifteen degrees out. People go ice fishing. People drive their cars on lakes. And besides, there was already a set of human tracks heading across the lake in just the direction that I needed to go. So …

I followed the tracks down to the edge of the lake. It was really a narrow part of the lake called Mammoth Creek, however it was still over a hundred feet across at that point. The ice appeared to be quite solid with about four to six inches of snow on top. The tracks led straight across with what looked like strong, confident strides. They were obviously made by someone larger than me. I, however, eased slowly out onto the ice. Each step that I took I looked, listened, and felt for any cracking, sinking, or any other possible indications that I could be heading into trouble, ready to turn and bolt back to shore at any moment. It was nerve wracking and excruciatingly slow going.

About halfway across, it dawned on me that it would have been a lot faster to have gone the long way around, but I was committed now. Looking around from the middle of the lake I could see no one in sight.

I was completely alone!

If I should fall in, there would be no one at all to help me. When they came looking for me, (*if* they came looking for me), all they would find would be a John-sickle, with fish nibbling my toes, stuck in the ice until the spring thaw!

How could I have been so stupid?!

But I wasn't being stupid! My logic was sound. I had carefully reasoned it out and proceeded with caution and awareness. I had made it this far without any indications of danger, so I continued cautiously the rest of the way across and made it safely to the other side.

Whew!

I took a look back at my crossing and thought to myself, "That wasn't so bad." I then turned north and headed toward the lodge, continuing to follow the same tracks, as they were going the same way I was. I followed the tracks up a small slope and through a stand of lodge pole pines, down and across a small meadow.

I wasn't too upset about having been left behind. I could take care of myself. I had had to become self-sufficient at an early age just to survive. And besides, I had an adventure story to tell when I got back to …

CRACK!!

"What the …?!"

I had sudden vertigo, a sinking feeling!

Looking around, it became suddenly obvious that the tracks I was following had led me, not through a meadow, but across an extension of the lake. A small bay!

I was back on ICE!!

Everything happened both fast and in slow motion. I was through the ice and into the freezing water! And, just as quickly, I hit the bottom of the lakebed. If this had happened to me now, my head would probably have been above water, but, at my height at that youthful age, it was up to my nose! Good thing it wasn't any deeper, but not good enough for me to get out!

A great deal goes through a person's head at a time like this.

"This is a funny way to die."

"Why didn't the ice break for that other guy?"

"Why did it break for me?"

"That was a pretty sneaky trick the lake pulled on me, pretending to be a meadow!"

"Do I have any options?"

"What would Bugs Bunny do??"

(Bugs had saved my life once before, but that is another story.)

I tried yelling, but that had the expected results. Nothing! I tried pulling myself out, but the ice just broke off at the edge.

Yet it didn't break easily enough that I could smash my way to shore before I froze to death.

What to do?!! I was frantic!

Things were getting a bit cold!

There must be some way, something!?

Anything?

No?

Well …

At least it was a beautiful place to go if it was one's time to go.

A strange calm came over me. I looked out at all the trees. I had always loved the pine forests. And the mountains. Nature had always called to me, as long as I could remember, and now it was calling me home! I looked up toward "Hole in the Wall," a cave-like thing up near one of the peaks to the west. I had always wanted to climb up there someday just to see what it was. Guess I may have missed my chance. I guess I'd missed my chance at a lot of things. I had never kissed a girl. Not really anyway. And I was just getting to the age that I was starting to want to! And making love! What was that all about? I had never even *been* loved! By anyone! Ever! I would sure have liked to have known what that was like.

Oh well …

I almost lazily looked around to the south and …

There!

There it was!

A hope!

My only hope!

There behind me on the ice sat my trusty sled!

All day it had followed me around like a loyal dog, and now, there it was, like Lassie to the rescue.

But I wasn't out yet. I had to somehow lever myself up onto the sled, and thus distribute my weight over a broader area of the ice, preventing it from cracking.

It was a chance, and I went for it.

With a full dose of adrenalin slamming through my blood stream, I dropped down and pushed off the lake bottom with all my strength. At the same time, I grabbed on as close to the midpoint of the sled as I could reach, and, as smoothly as I could, pulled myself up onto the sled. The water that had been splashed onto the snow packed in front of the runners, when I had first fallen through, had already frozen, making a nifty stop-block to keep the sled from coming toward the ice hole as I pulled on it. With a *whoosh*, I was out and half up on the sled. The ice crunched a little but held.

So far so good.

I reached further back on the sled and carefully pulled myself across and away from the hole.

I was all the way out!

Now, I needed to get to shore without breaking through again.

Pulling the sled free, I headed straight for shore, putting half my weight on the sled and pushing with the whole of my lower legs, my knees spread wide like a lizard. The weight-distribution trick worked, and in a few minutes, I was safely back on solid ground.

Slowly, I got up to my feet, shaky with cold and exhaustion. Looking back at the scene, I thought that the odd tracks I had left would make an interesting puzzle for any future passersby. I paused only for a second, because I had a very long, very cold walk ahead of me, and as they say, I quite literally wasn't out of the woods yet.

As quickly as I could muster, I made my way up to the road and the fastest way to the lodge. The heroic sled followed right behind me. I was not going to let go of that thing! Maybe not even in summer! Maybe not ever!

I proceeded down the road with natural haste but soon found that I was slowing down. Walking was getting more and more difficult. The reason became surprisingly obvious. I was developing an exoskeleton. I was becoming encased in ice!

Oh, will the challenges never end.

It was fifteen degrees out, that's Fahrenheit boys and girls, seventeen degrees below freezing! All the water I had brought with me since leaving the relative warm of the lake had been solidifying on me, from the outside in. I had become shiny and smooth. Now I knew how the "Tin Man" felt when rusting in *The Wizard of Oz*.

However, I soon noticed something else.

I was getting warmer.

I haven't said much about feeling icy cold because it would just be stating the obvious, but this early thawing was unexpected! I may have been crunchy on the outside but that hard cover was a great insulator, reflecting my body heat back onto me. And the physical effort that I was putting out to get back was warming me from the inside out. I was beginning to feel much better. No hypothermia for this kid!

By the time I sauntered up to the lodge, I was feeling quite normal. Wet, but normal.

As I approached the entry, cracking and crunching with every step, a lady was coming out. She let out such a cry that I turned around to see what was about to get me. Then I realized that I must be quite a sight. She turned back in the doorway and yelled something, and suddenly there was a tornado of activity. People were everywhere, grabbing at me, pulling me inside, and asking me questions. I only asked if my sled would be OK outside, and they just looked at me like, "Huh?" I was ushered into the bar where my father and uncle stood, drinks in hand, and they just stared with dull expressions as I related the story while other people tried to disentangle me from my ice cocoon.

I was stripped down, as much as modesty would allow, and, after my Uncle Jack, an M.D., declared "no frost bite," I was given a warm drink and made to stand on a large heating grate in the floor. I can still remember the sizzling sound it made as my melt water dripped through the grate onto the dusty heating unit, and the smell of the rising steam.

I don't believe that the experience affected me much. I still love snow and the beauty of winter. I even got into snow camping for a while. About the only thing I can think of that might be related is that I would go into a physical state of shock whenever therapists would put ice on my knees to reduce swelling after I had my legs rebuilt.

But that, of course, is a completely different story.

A PRACTICALLY PERFECT PRANK

Have you ever had a sudden inspiration that, when put into effect, came off like a charm?

I had, on one glorious occasion, the opportunity to almost experience such a moment. It happened one winter while visiting my uncle J.D.'s timeshare in Mammoth, "The Sierra Nevada Inn."

My parents, in an attempt to "keep-up" with my father's brother, had decided to learn to ski. For them, a hilarious disaster. They never got the hang of it, as proven by "The Skiing Movie," a family 8MM film of each of the adults repeatedly falling, over and over, while never traveling more than four or five feet at very slow, wobbling speed.

However, this minor sibling rivalry had an upside for me and my siblings. Seeing as J.D. had outfitted his kids with skis, my parents followed suite and outfitted us with the minimum requirements.

Unlike the adults, the kids took to the slopes like fish to water. This led to many skiing adventure stories of which this is not one! I'll save those for another time. I only seek to explain where we were and why we were there.

I think it was the year of the big snow. I remember being told that some places had received as much as fifty-two feet of snow. That's **feet** not inches.

Snow in the parking lot

I can still remember riding in the car on roads cut through the deep snow which towered high above us on each side. The snow strata on the sides varied in ever compressing layers from corn snow to powder and everything in between. Every so often, flush with the towering white walls like grotesque hieroglyphics, were the ripped-up sides of cars abandoned on the sides of the road during the first big snowstorm. They had been totally ravaged by snowplows that could not see them in the continually deepening snow.

At any rate, a lot of snow!

Now, after a hard day of running amok in the deep snow, we would return to the inn. It was at a slightly lower altitude, but still had a lot of snow. The inn was, and I guess still is, a lovely place to spend one's non-skiing time. Included in the amenities were a sunken fireplace infused with the fragrance of pine and oak wood smoke, surrounded by a wraparound cushioned seating area, a sauna room that smelled of cedar and "heat," a swimming pool and a good-sized hot tub. The indoor space always put me in mind of the ski lodge scenes from the original *Pink Panther* movie. However, it was the outside space that was the location of my high Sierra hijinks.

It had been a cold day's activities in the deep snow, and warm relaxation was in order. The parents were in the bar taking their warmth in liquid form, as was their all too regular custom. The younger set took to the hot tub.

Author with cousin in fateful hot tub

The pool and hot tub were just outside to the south of the lodge, set on a diagonal, with the tub to the southwest and the pool between tub and lodge. The pool's deep end was toward the lodge and the shallow end, with steps, closer to the rather large hot tub. There was a semi-circular shelter to the southwest of the tub, to block the cold winds off of the mountain, which sort of looked like a big hand cupping a very wet ear to better hear the pool! It started out with just five of us, four males and one female, but soon a few others joined in, all young and all in jovial moods. There was a lot of joking that led to bragging, that led to daring. We would dare each other to run out into the snow, dripping wet and clad only in our swimming attire. Each dare would take us in a loop ever farther from the warmth of the hot tub. The returning runner would then jump back into the hot tub, sizzling their freezing feet and splashing all the others. Oh, and there were a few snowballs thrown as well. A well-placed soft snowball impacting the bare skin of an unwary victim running barefoot through the snow, had a most satisfying result.

Unless you were the victim.

Which I was!

Perhaps this is what inspired me to seek my diabolical revenge.

By now the numbers of tub revelers had increased to ten. There were seven guys and three girls. Or, I should say that there were three girls for the seven guys to try to impress by doing stupid stunts.

A perfect idea was forming in my head, and the idea became a plan. The regular pool lay just a few feet away. Remarkably, for the amount of snow and cold, it was only about one third covered with ice toward the deep end. My guess is that the movement and warming caused by the circulating filter pump, was just enough to keep it from completely freezing over.

I put the plan into action.

Rising from the warmth of the hot tub, I announced loudly and confidently that, "It's too crowded in here. I'm going into the pool where there is more room!"

This statement was met with the expected guffaws and doubtful challenges. I stepped up out of the tub and strode toward the icy pond with the bravado of the ignorant. However, I was far from ignorant of what to expect. In fact, just a year previously, I had fallen through the ice into a frozen lake. I figured that I had a pretty good idea of what to expect. I had survived that, and I could survive this. And, if my plan worked, this time there would be a big payoff, well worth the momentary discomfort.

As my soon-to-be victims gleefully watched, waiting for me to turn back from what they were sure was a bluff on my part, I plunged down the steps, headlong into the icy pool, without a moment of hesitation.

Now, at this point, I must confess to a small flaw in my calculations. Last year, when I had become one with the lake, I had been wearing a lot of snow clothes. That had delayed the cold from touching me, and, to some extent, held in my body heat. Also, the effects of fear-induced adrenalin protected me from the sudden shock.

I had no such protections this time. The icy water wrapped around my bare body with full affect, causing every inch of my skin to scream its profound disapproval. Especially my minuscule man parts! My gonads slammed up into my body so hard I'd almost swear that they nearly came out my nose!

However, for this to work, I had to create the illusion of delightful comfort. So, summoning all my strength, and the skills I'd learned from a lifetime of hiding my pain, I leisurely rolled over on my back, gave a few casual back strokes, and said with a dreamy smile and an exhale of extreme contentment, "Ahhh! This is so much better!"

Can I act, or what?

Well, I guess I can because all but two of the girls and one guy jumped up en mass and lunged for the pool. More like the lemmings of legend than the lemmings themselves, they all at once flung themselves into the icy pool.

This was the payoff of a lifetime.

This was what I had subjected myself to some pretty serious discomfort to achieve!

And boy howdy was it worth it!

Because the moment that they splashed down into the pool, it was as though the water itself spit them straight out again! It was like somebody ran the film of them jumping in backwards! You've never heard such screaming and hollering and cussing, all the way back to the hot tub and even for some time after they got in it.

Well, what more can I say?

Insult received. Vengeance planned. Plan executed. Vengeance achieved without a single hitch. (If you don't count that I was by now a walking icicle!)

I casually rose up out of the pool and strolled over to the hot tub with an air of dignity and pride. Yeah, I was cold, very cold, but in a few seconds, I would be totally immersed in the nice hot water of the tub.

We interrupt this story with a science fun fact alert!

During the latter half of the twenty-first century, doctors and scientists performed experiments to understand the origins and nature of burn pain. They used a novel invention to test their theory. It consisted of two hollow tubes twisted around each other, like a unicorn's horn, which they had subjects hold firmly in their hands. They ran cold water through one tube and hot water the other. If they ran just the cold, the subject felt cold. If they ran hot, hot was felt. But, if they ran both hot and cold at the same time the subjects would drop the instrument, sure that they had been burned. You see, the simultaneous stimulation of both cold receptors and hot receptors in the skin is what creates the sensation of burning pain, even in the absence of actual fire.

And now, back to our story.

Where were we? Oh yes!

Cold, but not for long, I stepped through the grumbling hoard, and over the seat of the hot tub to the hot bubbling water in the deeper center of the tub, to totally immerse myself and thus warm up more quickly.

I won't even **try** to tell you the level and intensity of the resulting "ouch!" I will only say this: although it has been more than fifty years since that night, if you go out on some quiet windless night in the high Sierras, and the aroma of pine trees and wood smoke is in the cool air, and the light of a billion twinkling stars is dancing with the moonlight on the snowcapped mountain peaks, and if you listen, in the stillness, you can **still** hear the echoes of my scream.

A Ghostly Story

I don't believe in ghosts.

That being said, I have seen, and interacted with, them on several occasions.

These two statements may seem contradictory, and indeed they are, but the fact remains that they are also both true. I have seen, heard, and otherwise experienced many things that defy any other explanation other than what would be described as ghosts.

I should also make clear that I, very early on, became a follower of the empirical method of understanding the world. Thus, I will only relate those experiences that could be corroborated by witnesses who were carefully questioned in a way so as not to lead them toward or even let them know what I had seen. And yet, their experience was the same as mine.

My first witnessed account happened when I was a young, hormone-befuddled lad on the verge of manhood, about the age of thirteen.

Quite near my childhood home there were two houses referred to as the "haunted house" and the "murder house." They were on the same large plot of land, most of which was covered with long neglected orange trees.

The haunted house was a fairly standard three-bedroom house with a basement, at the southeast edge of the property, and was at one time the caretaker's house for the murder house.

The murder house was a once stylish mansion, on the top of a low hill at the center of the dilapidated orange grove, and quite isolated from the surrounding community. It, the story goes, had been built in the 1930s and had been owned by a succession of well-to-do bankers, Hollywood producers, and movie stars until it became the scene of seven murders and a suicide. An occurrence so notorious that, I was told, the house was the inspiration for the Vincent Price movie the *House on Haunted Hill.*

It was in the Fall of 1969. Men had walked on the moon. The police violence at Newport 69, (which took place on the property between the two houses mentioned above and my home) had inspired what would become known as "Woodstock." And my parents were putting on the last big party they would ever throw in the San Fernando Valley.

At this party, several guests brought their kids who were expected, like us, to stay quiet, stay out of the way, and behave, while the "adults" drank, and danced, and smoked till the wee hours. A naturally boring prospect for all of us not-quite-adults. As a group, we figured we could manage maybe one of the expectations put upon us, so we chose "stay out of the way." But where?

I believe it was my suggestion that we investigate the haunted house.

After my brother Jim's and my colorful description of the goings on there, all agreed. We headed out into the warm night, picking up a few neighbor kids on the way. A posse of ten or twelve enthusiastic, if not brave, young adventurers.

Now, the haunted house, as it was known, got its name because of the regular, even reliable, goings on there. Outwardly, the house appeared to be a fairly normal looking wooden house, set in a small group of large trees near what would have been a stream before it was lined with cement as most drainage ditches were in the valley. Inside, however, was another story. The house had been abandoned after a fire broke out in the basement and burned through the living room floor, through the ceiling, and made a skylight in the roof. Somehow, mattresses, cushions, and other soft fluff had found their way down the hole into the not too deep basement. Which was fortunate, because someone almost always ended up falling through the hole. Most of the kitchen appliances remained as they were, providing bells and buzzers that would go off on their own, even though there was no electricity in the house, at all! Doors and windows would slam shut, or open all by themselves, even though there was no wind. Creeks and groans and whispers seemed to come from everywhere. You can see why it was called the "haunted" house, and why it was irresistible to us kids.

Well, our kid posse, which ranged in age from about nine years old to a rather attractive seventeen-year-old named Judy, (I'll get to her later) headed west down our dusty dirt road in high spirits, through the dirt parking lot of the fairgrounds, and across the cement ditch that was the eastern perimeter of the murder house property, to the haunted house. The house did not disappoint.

Oh, what a gloriously spooky frolic!

How or why this house did what it did we never understood, and it really didn't matter. It never amounted to more than benign silliness. However, bells and buzzers went off. Doors and windows slammed and opened again sending kids scurrying in all directions. One kid fell out a window and no less than three kids fell through into the basement. We couldn't have been happier.

But even all this eventually grew tiresome, and we all withdrew from the house and set about making a new plan. As the waxing autumn moon was high, and so were our spirits, I made the outrageous suggestion that we go to "The Murder House." There was an instant, unanimous cheer of agreement. And then …

For what happened next my loyal followers can hardly be blamed. The murder house was something different, something more.

There really had been seven murders and one suicide there. That was a verifiable fact. I myself, had seen firsthand some of the evidence. Not at night. I had been there twice, in the full brightness of day with my brother and a friend. Once, we even went inside through a loose board nailed over a window. Immediately on entering we felt an almost overwhelming feeling of dread not like anything I could remember ever having felt before. There was an unpleasant smell of dust and rat droppings and death, as though some small animal had met its end there recently. Nevertheless, we wandered apprehensively through the large, almost empty rooms on the main floor, determined, as young boys often are, to see whatever there was to be seen. However, we only made it halfway down the basement steps. From that vantage point, even in the dim half-light filtering through the boarded-up windows, we could see what appeared to be human sized immutable blood stains soaked into the concrete floor! Filling our minds with images of the obvious mayhem that must have taken place on that fateful occasion, in this very house, we made a quick retreat and ran most of the way home.

At any rate, once we started toward the drainage ditch, one by one the, what had been intrepid adventurers, began to waffle and back out.

Now, my friends, I must confess not only didn't I blame anyone for not wanting to go. I was secretly in full agreement with them. After what I had experienced there in broad day light there was no way that I wanted to go near that place. And, at night?! I regretted it the moment that I suggested it. It is now that we come back to Judy.

As I mentioned, Judy was a seventeen-year-old girl, four years my senior. A woman really, and an attractive woman at that. She had been dragged to the party by her parents and only come with us out of boredom and because we were at least closer to her age than the adults. Now, take a pile of hormones parading around disguised as an inexperienced teenage boy, add an attractive girl, and no matter how smart he is, his IQ instantly takes a nosedive. I am absolutely sure Einstein did stupid things to impress some girl at some time. I may not be an Einstein, but I am also not an exception. I wanted to impress Judy. First with my great ideas and later with my apparent bravery. And so …

"I have to go and practice my accordion," said Billy. "It's late I'll get in trouble," said one of the other kids. "My parents will be wondering where I am," said another. One by one they all made weak excuses. But not me! I told them, "You cowards can go back if you want. I am going on to the murder house alone."

Brave huh?

No such thing. I'm no fool. I wasn't crazy. It was my plan to head up the ravine, up and around a corner, and there cool my heels for a while and then return with a wild story of ghosts and monsters and what-have-you. And thus become a local legend and a hero in Judy's eyes. (Hey, didn't I mention that I was thirteen at the time?) I played my role well though, and turning on my heel, headed off up the ditch with an impressive swagger.

The best laid plans …

I had just made it around the first bend when I heard someone call my name. It was Judy! Apparently, she, being the oldest, suddenly felt guilty letting a younger acquaintance go to meet his certain doom alone. She was going with me!

*@#%!!#@!!

Now there was no way out. I had to go.

Now, I wasn't afraid of no ghost. Not exactly anyway. But I had felt very uncomfortable in the house on that daylight occasion. I wasn't sure that I could get back into the house in the dark, and it was a bit of a hike to get there, perhaps half a mile. However, I was committed, and there was nothing to be done but get on with it. Thus, we proceeded up the ditch another couple hundred yards to a position roughly even with the house's position in the orange grove. We climbed up the steep concrete side of the ditch and began navigating through the grove. The trees had been planted in straight rows running north and south but alternating running east and west. I guess to best take advantage of the sunlight. As we were heading due west, our path undulated back and forth, like the path of a slalom skier.

I must say that for me this was not an altogether unpleasant experience. It was a relatively warm Indian summer night. The air was filled with scents of earth and dry grasses, and the pleasant smell of citrus permeated the grove. Crickets trilled and chirped their opinion that it was a night for romance. There was also the simple fact that I was alone in the woods, so to speak, with an attractive young woman. The waxing moon, lower now in the West, cast long dark shadows behind the orange trees, most of which were still living. There were a few small, light clouds that reflected the moon, as well as the ambient light of the surrounding San Fernando valley, giving us plenty of light to guide us on our journey, except when one of those mischievous clouds would fall across the face of the moon throwing us into temporary darkness. It was during one of these mini blackouts that things began to get a little more intense. As cliché as it sounds, and I swear this happened, as the darkness hit, ten feet in front of us, two cats started a small war! They then ran right past us causing us to jump into each other's arms. Judy held onto my arm the rest of the way up the hill. Thanks kitties.

From there on, the trees seemed to be closer. If you are familiar with orange trees then you know that they don't exactly have thorns, but they aspire to, and their branches seemed to claw at us. The sound of frogs ahead heralded our arrival out of the trees onto the open driveway, quite near the malevolent mansion, in fact, just outside the tall iron gate leading to the courtyard. Judy's grip tightened on my arm as we cautiously approached the unlocked gate.

Perhaps now would be a good time to describe the object of our quest and its surroundings. The mansion sat at the apex of the hill like an old fort. The only drive came in from the north to the gate at which we stood. An iron bar fence, shorter than the gate, surrounded the compound on three sides. The south side dropped away about ten feet, leaving a small patio space near the east end of the building and a drop exposing basement windows near the west end. To get to the building from the gate you had to cross a courtyard dominated first by a large fountain, a classic figure standing in a long-dry round pool with a raised wall, followed by a kidney-shaped swimming pool, stagnant rainwater in the deep end being the source of the frog song. The pool must have been added as an afterthought because it seemed more to block easy access to the main entrance to the house than compliment the landscaping. That was the thing about the whole house. Architecturally it just didn't work. It didn't have the harmony and balance of a Victorian, nor the flowing grace of Art Nouveau, nor the streamline of Art Deco. It was surely someone's great modern artistic idea, but it was square-ish and clunky and, in my mind, just plain ugly. In the movie the *House on Haunted Hill*, the house that they enter in the beginning of the movie is a fair, although infinitely more attractive, approximation of its look.

Now, our senses were all operating at their peak by the time we reached the gate. And as I slowly pulled it open it made a loud, long *Creeeeaak*! That was it for Judy. She had reached overload. She stopped in her tracks, and shaking her head, along with the rest of her, she stammered that she could go no farther. Nothing that I said could convince her to go further.

Good!

This created an opportunity to make a new plan. I would go alone around the back side of the house, cool my heels there and return with a good spooky story.

Now, I didn't really want to deceive, just entertain. It's not that I was afraid to go in the house, exactly. It's just, well, you know, it was dusty in there. I might get my clothes dirty. And I might, you know, get a splinter going through the boarded window. Uh, you know?

So, leaving Judy quivering at the gate, I bravely headed past the fountain, and around the deep end side of the dank smelling pool toward the eastern protrusion of the house. Just as I neared the corner, all the crickets and frogs suddenly stopped. So did I. Nothing. Not a sound! Not even a breeze rustling the leaves on the trees. Suddenly, Judy made a sound that I can't even describe. Something between a cry and a whimper. Looking back at her, I could even in the dim variable moonlight see the whites of her eyes wide with terror! Her frightened gaze as well as her trembling hand were directed toward the part of the L shaped building that was for me obscured by the nearby protrusion. I then made my way between the house and the pool to a position from which I could see the setback facade of the north wall. There I saw, through the broken, boarded up window into the main hall, that which so agitated my companion. From within the room there was a light. Were it today, one would guess that it was one of those chemical light sticks, the kind that you snap and shake, and it glows a weird alien green. Except such a thing wouldn't be invented for another decade or more. Well, this was weird all right, sinister, malignant. And it was moving!

At this point my natural scientific curiosity took over. What was this thing? Why did it glow? Why green?? I stepped toward the window. So did it!! It came closer and closer to the window. I stopped. It did not! It came right up to the window, glowing brightly behind the boards, somehow changing shape. It came onward. Through the boards! It seemed to extrude between the boards, like Jell-O being forced through a screen. Separating and then recombining on the other side. And then there it was. On my side of the window. Hanging there. Gaseous, about the size of a man but with no discernible shape. And not touching the ground! At that point, Judy screamed.

Remembering I had a friend at the gate, and feeling no need to make a new one here, I spun on my heel and took off. I ran back around the pool, past the fountain, through the gate, and grabbing Judy with my left hand, proceeded at top speed into the orange grove, never stopping to look back.

By now the few small clouds had multiplied into almost a buttermilk sky, the moonlight alternating dark and light. Cutting corners for speed while running the slalom trail back, I ran into a long-dead orange tree with my right side. The tree grabbed firmly onto the sleeve on my right arm. Being in no mood to tarry, and being quite charged with adrenalin, I continued on unimpeded, snapping the over-familiar tree off at its moldering roots and carrying it along several yards before extricating myself from its grip. Together we ran. We ran through the grove. We ran down the cement embankment. We ran down the drainage ditch. We did not stop running until we were halfway across the fairgrounds parking lot, and out in the clear open, and then we stopped. We stopped and panted and tried to catch our breath, and to comprehend what had just occurred.

I knew quite clearly what I had seen, then, as clearly as I do now. But what had Judy seen? I asked her, being very careful not to give any hint as to what I had experienced. Her account, except for the different perspective which included me, was exactly the same as mine. That is how I know that the experience was real. What we saw **was** real! What it **was** that we saw I don't know. I didn't then, and I don't now.

We returned to my home and the party crowd. We told our story, and it was met with skepticism and chiding, even after showing them my scratches and torn sleeve. I guess our true story was more outrageous than the one I planned to make up. But I swear to you, on all that I hold dear, that what I have told you **is the truth.**

Well, soon afterward, my family moved away to San Diego. I never returned to the murder house. However, I did see Judy again. In fact, she came to San Diego and lived with us for a time. She was the first girl I ever saw in a filmy "ghost-like" baby doll nightie, and the first girl I ever open-mouth kissed.

But, that is a completely different story.

The Flood of '78

In what must have been early in the year of 1978, at least I am pretty sure it was 1978, because I was working as a bartender during the event (although I don't drink and didn't at the time, but that is another story). There were record rainfalls that resulted in flooding throughout San Diego County.

I was living in Santee at the time. The San Diego River pretty much bisected Santee as it ran from east to west. As the river was normally not much more than a trickle, there were no bridges across it, just low culverts under the road. If we experienced anything more than a normal rain, the river would cross the road, making it challenging to get out of the bedroom communities.

On this occasion, it had rained steadily for a couple of weeks (although not quite forty days and forty nights). The river had risen, making the road crossing the river between my house and town almost impassable. But it was a steady flow. For this short time, Santee had an actual lovely little river running through it, complete with ducks and geese.

It was my brother Jim's idea to take a three-man inflatable raft—that he had obtained in one of his obscure bartering deals—and go out for a ride down the river. As it was a beautiful day, this sounded like a grand idea.

We gathered our supplies, including the paddles that I had made out of wood, (mine sporting eyes I had painted on the lower part so it could "see" what was going on under the raft) as none came with the raft, and headed out to the Cuyamaca Street Bridge, the one bridge that actually crossed over the river, further to the east in Santee. We had left one car where the river crossed Carlton Hills Boulevard to the west, so that we would have a way back to where we left the first car. We were quite proud of ourselves for thinking of this.

With the meanderings of the newly inflated river, this gave us around a half a mile or more of leisurely boating before getting out at Carlton Hills. You would not want to cross Carlton Hills in the raft as this led immediately into the dense forest that preceded the golf course and even at our leisurely pace, that could be, shall we say, problematic.

When we set out for our first run, a small group of people that had gathered to observe the rare sight cheered us on from the bridge as we intrepidly paddled beneath. We had even dressed the part of explorers, Jim wearing his leather frontiersmen coat with the fringe to wick away water, and I wearing my current favorite of my hat collection, the leather cap with the fur fringe that he had bought me in Mexico.

The sun occasionally broke through the clouds and made everything sparkle as we slowly floated without a care in the world. The friendly little waterway was up to fifty feet wide in some places. In others it narrowed where it bent around taller obstacles in its path and had bumpy little ripples that gave one the sense they were riding on a gentle little pony.

A little less than halfway down our river run was a most pleasing challenge in the form of a stand of trees, mostly tall trunked eucalyptus and a few scraggy willows that, normally not being bothered by any water to speak of, had grown into a dense little forest following the path of the river. One had to do some pretty fancy paddling to avoid bumping into a tree trunk, but it mattered little if you did, as you would just gently bump the tree and the slow-moving water would just slowly spin you around and send you on your way.

On exiting the little forest there was a sudden jog to the left and a small drop as the little river butted up against some kind of old retaining wall that preceded a change of elevation of about five or six feet creating the only notable rapid on the trip as it meandered around the hazard.

What followed then was about 100 yards of open space where the water spread out and slowed down a bit before crossing Carlton Hills Blvd. and plunging into the dark and dangerous forest of dread.

Oh, what a beautiful little journey. The fresh smell of the water carrying the scents of exotic plants from far upstream. The glorious golden sun skittering in and out of the dramatic silver lined clouds and glittering upon the rippling water. The ducks and geese that seemed to accept us as one of their own and float alongside us as we lazily drifted down the gentle waterway. Oh, what a lovely, lovely time. This was an experience that must be shared!

After Jim and I ran the river twice, we returned home and I immediately started calling friends. Being a weekday, available people were hard to come by. However, I did reach my former first true love, and then and now best friend, Barby. She had to work that night but thought that her sister Sandy and her then husband Neil would be around. This was perfect. They lived close by and between me and the river. I called them and within fifteen minutes was back at the river. Jim had to go into his bartending job, so I took Sandy for a run down the river in our raft. She must have had a pretty good time because they went right out and bought a surprisingly inexpensive raft of their own.

Another hour passed and we were once again at the bridge, this time with two rafts, one brand new with plastic paddles. The group on the bridge had grown into a small crowd and seemed just as excited to see us launch as the first group had been. There were waves and cheers and envious comments as we slid the rafts into the swirling waters, me in the lead with Sandy and Neil following close behind, and we cruised under the concrete structure and out into the open river. What a joyful adventure we were on. It was later in the afternoon and the clouds were a little darker to the east, but the wind was calm, and we still had plenty of golden sunlight, so it all seemed very peaceful and grand.

And then, it began to change.

Perhaps, looking back, the first sign of trouble should have been the commotion on the bridge. There was a lot of hollering and waving that we just took to be another round of approval of our heroic spirits. In retrospect, it had a more ominous meaning.

I first became aware of an increase in the volume of the ambient noise in our surroundings. We had to yell louder to hear each other from one raft to another. Also, we seemed to be rising up, an odd sensation to say the least. What finally clued me in, and raised alarm within me, was our sudden increase in speed. The meaning of it all slammed me like a Mack truck hitting a butterfly on the freeway.

FLASH FLOOD!
But, how??

No time for speculation, I yelled back to the unaware Sandy and Neil, "We're in trouble!!"

What had been a gently rolling stream was suddenly a roaring, swirling, raging torrent much wider than a moment ago, the shore getting further away in both directions. In a matter of seconds, we were moving at three times our previous speed.

The ride was rougher but still manageable for the moment, but we were quickly approaching the dense little forest. Difficult to navigate at the slow gentle speed, was it even possible now? And I really didn't want to know what would happen if the raft should impact a tree at this crazy speed.

I hollered back to S and N to stay close and follow me in. Not too difficult as we were riding the same current. The trees came. Sparse at first, then a few more. Then more and more. Paddling like crazy, first right then left, just missing one tree then grazing the next. I was aware when the raft S and N were in scuffed over the top leaves of a willow slowing them slightly for a moment and putting them farther behind me. There was little I could do for them now. Things were bad!

I had no idea just how bad, but I was to find out promptly. That quick glance over my shoulder at S and N was just enough to throw me off my rhythm. As I turned forward again, I ran headlong smack into a tree. From there, so much happened so fast. The impact was a jarring blow. So much so that my hat flew off into the water to one side of the raft. I clearly remember watching my much-loved hat spinning and sinking into the murky violent water. I began to reach for it but stopped as it dawned on me that, with what was about to happen to me, it wasn't really going to matter anymore.

I will try to describe what happened in the next two seconds as accurately as I can …

As I hit the tree, the bow of the raft was shoved slightly down along the trunk of the tree. I bounced off of the tree and landed toward the aft of the small vessel. My weight drove the stern down where it was caught by the overwhelming pressure of the flood water which slammed it down full length along the length of the trunk. I, too, was plastered by the tremendous water pressure, and by a quirk of luck, head up, back to the raft and the tree, my head at least a full foot and a half beneath the water.

Thoughts raced through my mind. "Damn that is a lot of pressure! What if a log or something smashes into my face?! How do get out of this?!"

One thing I knew for sure was there was no air down there. I had to get to the surface fast.

I tried to move my arms.

I couldn't!

I tried to push up with my legs.

I couldn't move at all against the pressure!!

It very soon became obvious that this was it! Game over.

I never felt any real panic. It was just, well, the end. We, all of us, wonder what might go through our minds in that final moment. I very clearly remember thinking, "What a stupid way to die!"

But then, there was another thought.

Sandy and Neil are still up there.

And they are going to die too.

And it is my fault they are here!

Something in me changed. Somehow my strength grew. My arm moved!

Slowly, I slid my right arm up along the raft and trunk, up and out of the water. Somehow, I found a branch to grasp. With more strength than I could possibly have, I pulled myself up and up, against the raft, the tree, and the water pressure until my head popped out and I was once more in the land of the living and breathing. At least temporarily.

I came up just in time to see S and N rush by about fifteen feet to my left both clinging to their overturned raft, paddles gone, and totally at the dubious mercy of the frigged waters. They were in trouble but at least they were still alive. A welcome sight to see, albeit a brief one, as they soon disappeared into the thicket of trees.

I had to save them.

But first things first. I had to somehow dislodge the raft from the tree. Pulling myself the rest of the way out of the water and up into the tree, I jumped down onto the pinned raft, jarring it loose. The bad news was that the raft came up upside down. The good news was that I had had the foresight to tie my paddle to the raft with a long string, and it was still with me.

Riding on the underside of the little raft and paddling like a crazy person, I lurched right and left, managing to avoid any more serious tree collisions all the way through the little forest.

Almost!

Just as I was almost clear, one of the last few trees snagged me, spinning me backwards into the next tree with similar results to the first major hit, with the exceptions that my head and shoulders were above water and this time I was caught between the raft and the tree. To make matters much worse, the waters were now quite deep, so I was about fifteen feet up in the tree, where it was branching off in a v shape. A two by four, or something like it, had caught across the v and my leg below the knee was caught between that and the current-mashed raft. The pressure wasn't quite enough to break my leg, thankfully, however I was very securely, and painfully, pinned.

My new situation had good news and bad news. The good news was that I had slammed to a stop not thirty feet from S and N. They, still clinging to their raft, had washed up with some other flotsam near the bushy top of a submerged willow tree and were, for the time being, relatively safe. The bad news was that, as I have said, I was pinned tight, and the water was rising.

S an N looked pretty wide-eyed and frightened. Quite understandable under the circumstances, but not very helpful. So, I hollered over to them, "See, didn't I tell you this would be fun?"

After a moment, staring at me open-mouthed, they both broke into laughter, and the fear spell was broken. We joked back and forth a bit and then set about planning our escape from the flooded river. As they were in a fairly secure position and had no paddles, I, still in possession of my trusty paddle, would make a break for land and affect their rescue from there. Now all I had to do was not drown and free myself and my raft.

This first part of the plan was proving problematic. The water was now up to my chin. Inch by inch the water continued to rise, and the "bear trap" holding my leg was showing no sign of letting go. Now this is the point where someone always comes to the rescue, right? It would be a great time to see Superman, or in this case Aquaman, or Wonder Woman, or hell, even Dudley Do-Right! Anybody! I guess life really isn't like the movies. In most cases we have only ourselves and our wits to rely on. However, I didn't want S and N to have to carry that burden, so I had to keep up a brave face. And, at this point, that was all there was left of me to see. I hung there, my head tilted back to keep my nose out of the water, smiling like an idiot so as not to alarm my nearby companions, desperately seeking some advantage over the forces of nature, when I caught a break. As I was getting deeper under water, so was the inflatable raft, and it didn't like it any more than I did. The raft gave a sudden small shift upward allowing me just enough time and space to rip my leg free. I then used the board that was once my captor to stand on and hoist myself out of the water onto a branch.

Well, I was back in business. All I had to do was dislodge the raft from the tree and I'd already done it once. From my new, slightly higher, position, I could clearly see what lay ahead. I would head out of the last trees, past a very small island, past the rapids, cross the wide-open straightaway, and try to reach the shore before the flood crossed the road into the woods. There were just two problems. The first was that what was a little jog into a small rapid was now a roaring waterfall where the much deeper water poured over the wall into a kind of pit. I watched in awe as a good-sized log heading down stream went over the falls into the roiling whirlpool of foam and didn't come up! I had only one shot. If I followed roughly the original course, jogging left, and I could hit the edge of the whirlpool just right, the added momentum just might sling me clear of the danger.

Well …

I made my farewell to S and N once more, assuring them that I would be back. Then, with two hard drops down onto the raft, I dislodged it, this time right side up with me and my paddle properly in it. I paddled hard and fast, with laser focus on that far edge of the whirlpool. The little raft bucked and lurched like a bronco trying to throw me off. When I went over that final drop it felt like I was going to just keep going down, right through the bottom of the raft. I bounced up, spinning all the way around 360 degrees. Then, as if to admit it had lost this round, the water flattened out smooth. I had made it. I had hit the whirlpool just right, and for the third time in less than half an hour, had cheated death!

Well, now for the second of those two problems.

I was about in the middle of the swollen river. It was more than two-hundred-feet to reach land on either side. I had maybe three-hundred-feet before hitting the forest of death, and the raging flood water was moving fast! Really fast! If I hit that next set of trees, there was no way that I could cheat death a fourth time. If I couldn't get to the shore in time the Grim Reaper would at last have his prize.

I lit out straight for the north shore paddling like a windmill in a tornado. Even so, I was going sideways faster than I was forward. I pushed even harder, to the very limit of my strength, breathing so hard it felt like my lungs were on fire and going to burst any second.

And then my paddle hit something.

It hit it again!

I had gotten close enough to shore that the water was only a little more than a foot deep. I threw myself out of the raft, still holding onto the rope that ringed it. My feet were on solid ground for the first time in what seemed like forever.

However, my adventure wasn't over yet. I still had two friends clinging on for their very lives out there in the flood.

I slogged the rest of the way to dry land as fast as I could, working on a rescue plan the whole way. I dragged the raft up a safe distance from the waters edge. As I was hurriedly untying the rope from the raft, a pickup truck with huge tires and long antennas rolled up on the vague dirt road behind me. Nobody had cellphones in those days, but those antennas meant that the people in that truck had a CB radio. I ran to the truck and filled in the occupants as to my friends' situation and told them to call for help. Then, not knowing whether help would get there in time, or at all, and taking the short rope, I ran upriver toward the approximate position I had left S and N. I knew they had been in the trees several yards east of the small island and I could see the island from my position on the shore. Moving upstream to where I felt they were, plus a bit more, as I anticipated being shoved down stream some by the fast current, I hesitated for a moment. Was this the best course to take? After all, I had only just barely escaped with my life. Was it wise to head back into danger? I could just wait for help to come. But that was just it, help may not come, and I had two people in great jeopardy out there!

I plunged in.

Slogging first through the shallows, then ever deeper. The deeper I got the harder the flood pulled against me. I could feel The Reaper looking over my shoulder. It is nice to be wanted, but not by this dark spirit.

On I pushed, not sure I could reach them, but I had to try. Waist-deep, I could see them now, higher up on the bush-like tree, but still alive. I don't know if they ever saw me, but just as they came into view, there was the sound of thunder overhead. It was the sheriff's helicopter. The CB radio people had gotten an emergency call through.

The green-and-white helicopter had already been in the air close by. As there was no wind or rain, they were on a routine flight. (No wind or rain? Then why the flash flood?) It now circled around overhead surveying the situation. Suddenly, a voiced boomed from the sky, like the voice of God. It advised me to, "Head back to shore. (They) had this."

So, not being one to challenge the law … (OK, well not when we were both trying to rescue somebody, and they had a helicopter and all I had was a little ten-foot rope!) I backed away toward the north shore. Not all the way though. I wanted to be close in, just in case.

Their plan was a bold one. They called down to the stranded rafters and told them to hang onto the raft and kick off and float to the little island, about thirty feet directly downstream from their treetop location. They, after a bit of organizing, complied and successfully achieved the small island. Now when I say small island I'm not kidding. This thing was a short bump no more than six-feet by eight-feet, if that. So, what happened next was nothing short of amazing.

The helicopter slowly lowered down and down until it just touched the tip of one runner on top of the point of land. I then watched as Sandy, after a bit of hesitating and gesturing, rose out of the water and boarded the right side of the aircraft. The chopper then quickly rose up and over my head to a clearing about fifty yards away and deposited the dripping damsel on dry land. As the pilot took the craft up and over me again, I slogged my way back to shore and by the time I got there, Sandy was there to meet me.

Her first words to me were, "This is so embarrassing, let's run!"

That we may well have done but for the spectacle still playing out mid-river.

But "why embarrassing?" you say. You see, Neil was at that time, and for the past year or so had been, a deputy sheriff! He was about to receive a ribbing for this for now, and for years to come.

We watched as the whirlybird again touched down on the island and watched as another animated dialog took place. Eventually, Neil reluctantly let go of the raft on its maiden voyage. The down-blast from the massive fan above gave it a little extra kick on its way until it went over the falls, disappearing for a long moment only to pop up past the whirlpool. It then picked up speed, and before the helicopter could even fly its former captain to land, it had crossed the road into the forest never to be seen again.

Well, the sheriff's copter dropped the damp deputy sheriff off on land and had to head to another emergency elsewhere, leaving no time for questions. The three of us, with a long look back at the river, gathered my raft, and headed to the car and home.

Of course, the daring rescue of a man and a woman made the TV news and the newspapers. No names were given, nor even a mention of a doofus with a rope making a valiant attempt.

One ignorant paper went so far as to state "There is no law against stupidity." I, for one, agree with their implication that there should be accountability for this incident. But not for the intrepid adventures. For, as it turns out, the reason for the flood was because, at a large dam upstream, the bureaucrats in charge decided it was fuller than they wanted it to be, so they, with total disregard for any problems it may cause downstream, literally opened the floodgates. Stupidity indeed!

As for the traumatized victims, after losing their new raft and almost more, were they scarred for life? You be the judge. That very week they went out and bought a bigger raft.

A Fish Named Fluffy

In life, sometimes we'll come up against an individual that impresses us, teaches us, profoundly changes our way of thinking. Sometimes it is a great hero or leader. Sometimes it is a teacher or perhaps honored relative.

Sometimes it's a fish.

My ichthyologic enlightenment took place at one of the busiest times of my life. I was going to college, as well as being employed there professionally as a teacher and director/choreographer (which included lighting design, music direction, and costume design and manufacture). Additionally, I was supporting myself by working as a ceramic tech for a pottery business, a jeweler at a shop doing repairs as well as original works in gold and silver, running my own stained-glass business, and I was the area's foremost expert in antique glass window restoration. In addition to all that, I was teaching ceramics, folk dancing, and drama through parks and rec., performing with three dance troops including my own, and, in my spare time, creating art. I even had a social life with friends and even a girlfriend.

One day while perusing some ads that came in the mail, I came upon a coupon from a local pet store for five free goldfish. Seeing as I already had an old fishbowl sitting in the garage, I thought, "Why not, this could be fun."

In short order I picked up my five new friends, and after a brief, undignified ride in a plastic bag of water with a rubber-band to keep their mobile environment intact, they arrived at their new home, a one-gallon clear glass fishbowl with two round sides and two flat sides for maximum fish viewing.

There were two orange goldfish, a mottled gray one, an almost white one, and one fish, closer to gold in color with a distinctive lighter-colored spot on its left side.

This last fish stood out from the others right away. He, although slightly smaller than the others, seemed bolder, smarter. I say 'he' because, for some reason, I got a male vibe from him. The others would follow him around in their miniature portable lake, and he in turn would seem to follow me around. He always seemed to be interested in what I may be doing.

So, what do you name a fish like that? Bold, smart, shiny gold with a prominent spot … so, I named him "Fluffy."

Life with the fish became routine. Whenever I got home at night, I would feed them and watch them for a while. It was relaxing and would help me calm down after a very busy day. Almost every morning I would put their bowl in the kitchen sink and let the water run into it for a bit to clean the bowl and freshen the water. Then, I would leave for the day and the fish would have the house to themselves.

One particularly busy day, I was in a hurry to leave and so had to rush my routine a bit. I put the fishbowl in the sink, turned on the water and left it while I finished gathering what I needed for the long day. I came back, turned off the water, put the bowl on the counter and was out the door.

It was twelve hours before I returned home that day. I brought in all my stuff, put away the groceries, and sat down to rest and de-stress for a long minute. Not for too long however because I had mouths to feed. I picked up the fish food, walked to the counter and stopped short. Something was wrong! There were only four fish in the bowl. Fluffy was missing!!

Tired as I had been, I was now wide awake. What could have happened? Where could Fluffy be? He hadn't run away. There was no note, and the car keys were still there. I had to think. The sink!

I rushed to the kitchen sink and looked, fearful of what I might see. No dead fish. The sink was empty. Or was it? Something made me look again. There, down in the drain, something moved. What I saw thrilled and horrified me at the same time. The kitchen sink had two sides, one with a garbage disposal, the other just a drain, lacking the little basket for catching stuff before it goes down the drain. All it had was the little cross that keeps out the big stuff. And there. There was little Fluffy. Barely hanging on one of those crossbars by the very tip of one of his gill flaps! That little goldfish had been hanging there, by his gill flap, out of water, over the black maw of certain death, for more than twelve hours.

And he was still ALIVE!

How the … ?!

That was amazing and wonderful, but now I had a big problem. How the heck was I ever going to get him out of there?

The whole fish was already down in the drain, all except for the very tip of his gill cover. Understand boys and girls, he wasn't caught or stuck or wedged in any way, just hanging there, like if you were hanging by your earlobe. The slightest movement and he would drop into the abyss, never to be seen again. Somehow, he must have sensed the danger and held perfectly still. If he had flapped or flipped even once he would have been a goner.

As mind-boggling as the scientific and philosophical implications of all this were, getting Fluffy out alive was still the immediate concern. Firstly, I had to avoid an instinctive panic response to just reach in and try to grab the little creature. The sink hole was far too deep and narrow to effectively get my big primate fingers into. Forcing calm, I reasoned that I needed just the right tool. Something long with a small clamping surface and just the right curve near the end. I ran to my garage workshop where I found the perfect tweezers in among my jeweler's tools and was back in a flash. With full concentration and the steady hand of youth, I proceeded with the delicate operation.

There was a small gap of not quite 2mm between the part of the gill that hung up on the drain and the main body of the fish that I had to hit on the first try to be successful. Holding my breath, I carefully plunged the tweezers down into the yawning maw of the drain and then abruptly at a right angle adeptly sliding the tip into the necessary gap. Giving a light squeeze, I gripped the gill cover and, with a gasp of relief, lifted the wee beast out of the drain and out of the immediate danger it posed.

The next challenge became quite obvious. The little fella was very dry. He was drier than I have ever seen a living fish before or since.

He was like a little golden corn chip, curled slightly to the left. However, by a stunning show of strength of will and sheer determination, he was still breathing, in spite of having been traumatized and hung out in the air for more than twelve hours. I say it again because I am still amazed! HOW!!? The only thing I can figure is that the air in the drain was humid enough that the gills still had some minor functionality.

I knew that I had to get water flowing over those gills fast, and from the look of Fluffy he wasn't going to be doing any fast swimming any time soon. So, still hanging onto his gill flap with the tweezers, I held him underwater in the fish tank and began moving him back and forth through the water face first, getting plenty of flow through his mouth and over his gills.

Five minutes passed and he was moving his fins a little.

Ten minutes and he began to flex his body back and forth a bit.

Fifteen minutes and he was moving well enough that I could let him go and he was moving on his own. Not fast and not straight but roughly forward. He was still bent to the left, so he tended to go in circles, but moving and breathing he was.

He continued to swim bent for the next three days, but he did eventually get back to his funny, feisty self. What a big adventure for such a little fish.

Quite an adventure it was, and that could be a happy ending to this story, but there is more!

Fluffy and I kept company for almost two more years. By that time the gang in the bowl had been reduced to two, one of the orange ones—not very notable in personality so we'll just call him Goldie—and the mighty Fluffy. This was not *due* to any more major fish misadventures or lack of care on my part but to, I'm told, natural attrition. You see, the type of goldfish they usually give away in such promotions as I received my little buddies from are called feeder fish. They are not bred for longevity, but for large numbers. They just need to live long enough to become a meal for other, bigger, more expensive fish. By cheap fish standards, these two had beat all the odds and achieved a goldfish golden old-age.

It was at this time that things in my own life started going exceedingly badly and my own mortal existence became in question. I had one of my favorite knee joints completely blow-out on the job, and got caught in the workman's comp system, the most horrible, degrading, demeaning, and dysfunctional piece of crap system in the world! After years of fighting with them, when I finally got the surgery I needed, their insurance hack doctor did experimental surgery on me without my permission, messing up my leg badly. It ruined my dance career and life plan, caused me to become homeless for more than a year, and lose most of, who I thought were, my friends. I was told that I might never walk again, and even if I did, I would never make it to sixty-two years of age without being confined to a wheelchair. It caused me almost a decade of intense physical and mental agony!

But I digress. At any rate, there came a time when I could see the writing on the wall, as they say, and I knew there would be troubled times ahead where even caring for some little fish might be too difficult. So, I decided to set them free.

Now, you must understand that this was a time before it was generally considered a bad thing to release pets into the wild, and so, that was not a deterrent. Although now it would be unthinkable.

I chose a place that I dearly loved. A place that I wouldn't mind living if it were possible. A place we simply called "the canyon."

I've looked down from space and seen that it miraculously still exists. However, I'll decline to give away its exact location because everyone I know that has ever been there came away with the number one priority of keeping it wild and pristine.

Let me give you an example: on one occasion, a friend and I had the very, very rare experience of running into other people there. It was a couple of bad biker dudes. The rough type that looked as if they might kill their own mother just for the fun of it. How they had found their way over the two mountains, past the abandoned goldmine, and into the valley I don't know, but they were there, and they had seen us and now one was heading our way. We braced ourselves and prepared for action! (That most probable action being running away as fast as we could and screaming like little girls.) At any rate, we held our ground as the ruffian approached. He faced us, and with a soft, almost reverent, voice greeted us and asked if he might ask us a favor. He had noted that we had backpacks, and as he did not, asked if we might carry out a couple of empty beer cans, if it were not too inconvenient, as he had only his bare hands and it was inconceivable to leave trash in such a beautiful place. We were only too happy to oblige.

The author precedes friend Dave down one of "the canyon's" water slides

Anyway, through the bottom of this spectacular valley ran a year-round stream. It meandered for about two miles, from pool to pool, over and through huge granite rocks creating waterfalls and rapids. Traveling from the high flat plains at one end and ending by going over an un-scalable, couple-hundred-foot cliff in a beautiful cascading waterfall at the other.

This is where I chose to part with my shiny little friends.

After carefully transporting them the miles, over, down, and through, I chose a large pool a few hundred feet above the big waterfall. A pool that I knew well from the many times that we went fishing there. Yes, one of the great joys of the canyon was in the many lovely afternoons we spent there catching the numerous wild fish, mostly bluegill and pumpkin seeds, and very carefully letting them go after giving them a stern lecture on the evils of lure biting. One thing for sure, Fluffy and Goldie would not have to be alone.

Over the hard months that followed, it occasionally gave me a small bit of comfort to think of the brave little water wiggler adventuring along the stream and through the ponds, surrounded by all that natural beauty. And I dreamed of the day when I could walk well enough to return to the canyon.

Remembering the strength and courage of the little fish gave me inspiration to overcome my difficulties. And so, although "They" had made me a cripple, "I" was determined "not" to stay one!

And so it was.

It was a year-and-a-half before I got back on my feet, both literally and figuratively, enough to be able to return to the canyon. It was slow and painful crossing the two mountains, passing the abandoned goldmine, and descending into the valley below, with a metal brace painfully clamped onto my right leg like an angry alligator. However, it was so worth the effort to be surrounded by all that natural beauty and solitude once again.

It was the sights, sounds, and smells of the wilderness environment that brought me back. It was not to search for the little fish. For, after all, how could such a tiny little, short lived, feeder fish survive in the wild for a year-and-a-half? However, as long as I was there already, I wandered down to the pond where I'd last seen him.

The water ran calmly through the backyard swimming pool-sized pond, smooth and clear. So clear, in fact, that it looked like a window into another world. I stood there for some time, gazing at the serene surroundings: listening to the soft gurgling sound of the little stream tumbling over the granite rocks into the pool; smelling the fresh sent of the clean water and the lush vegetation of the riparian environment; fulfilling a need that I had nearly forgotten during my long, painful, convalescence and exile from nature; a truly beautiful, peaceful place. I thought "If the little fish had to go, at least …"

Suddenly, there was a commotion to my right! Something underwater shooting across towards the left. Something so big and moving so fast that it pulled the surface of the water down, creating a wake behind it. A fish! A big one. A big golden fish, with a light-colored spot on its left side. There could be no mistake. It was Fluffy! And he was huge! My little one-and-a-half-inch friend was now at least seven-and-a-half, eight inches long! He had not only survived, he'd thrived. And he was not alone. He had an armada of pumpkin seeds, half his size, with him, respectfully following his lead.

Fluffy was the boss of the pond!

I left the canyon that day never to return. After that last trip, people put in avocado groves along the access road and fenced the whole area in, blocking the trail.

I've lived a full adventuresome life since then, with both good times and bad. And when things get really rough, and I feel like quitting, I persevere by thinking of Fluffy, the little fish with an indomitable will, and a courageous heart as big as all outdoors.

The Case of the Reluctant Pilot, Or, My Other Car Is a Nuclear Aircraft Carrier

I have always had a keen interest in flight. Birds, planes, rockets. All manners and means of flying. To rail against the mighty grip of gravity. To defy the invisible powers that bind us to the earth and soar in ultimate freedom, high above the mundane. Even now, if I must fly on a commercial jet from one place to another, I get a window seat, and day or night, marvel at the view of the planet speeding by far below.

I wanted to learn to fly a plane. I was told, when quite young, that one could take lessons and obtain a pilot's license at the age of sixteen, and I would have done just that had I the means and the opportunity. Which I did not. So, I did not.

Perhaps, then, with this in mind, one can imagine the mix of feelings I had when I was put in a situation where I had little choice but to take a small aircraft through takeoff, flight, and landing, at night mind you, without the benefit of any lessons.

It wasn't my fault.

How could such a thing happen, you say? Well, it was orchestrated by quite a character of a person, who, at the time, was a good friend of mine, almost like a brother. In fact, for a short time, he, officially at least, was my brother. Or, more precisely, I was his.

This will take a bit of explaining, and it is a bit of a digression, but I think to tell the story will shed some light onto the thought processes of this individual.

For the purposes of privacy, and to avoid getting anyone into trouble, even though all this happened almost three decades ago, let's just call this fella B. I got to know B through conversations we had at "Jitterbug Club," a weekly dance that wasn't actually a club nor was jitterbug the only dance they did, but it was one of my primary social outlets and generally a lot of fun being had by a lot of friendly people. It was also a great place to meet the ladies and one thing B and I had in common was, we both liked to meet the ladies. We began mutually attending other gatherings as well, and through the repeated contact developed a friendship.

One of the non-dancing events that B would invite myself and other friends to was an annual air show at the local Naval Air Base. It turns out that B was a man of some accomplishment in the Navy, and he was attached to a local fighter wing at the air base. You may have heard of it, it went by the name of "Top Gun." Yeah, *that* "Top Gun." So, when we would watch the air show it was from on the tarmac, among the pilots not currently in the air.

B was always coming up with ideas of interesting things to do. But none as interesting as an unusual offer he made through a letter I received from him while he was away with the fighter wing in the Persian Gulf just at the end of the Gulf War. He offered me a ride from Hawaii to Bremerton, Washington on a nuclear aircraft carrier.

Okay, uh, Say *what*?

Yeah. You heard right. Just a leisurely cruise from HI to WA, for a week on a super massive, bad ass, nuclear aircraft carrier.

All I would have to do was get myself to Honolulu, stick out my thumb, and they would pick me up! Should I go for it?

Hell Yeah!!

All right, it was a little more complicated than that. You see, the navy has a thing called a "Tiger Cruise." When a deployed ship is finally homeward bound, the navy personnel are permitted to have their immediate male (that was then, it may be different now) relatives join them for the final leg of their journey. Pretty cool, huh? A great tradition. One small problem however, I wasn't even remotely related to B.

Now B was a very clever and resourceful fella. One with many contacts, connections, methods. A man with relationships, knowledge, and opportunities. So, he devised a complex, ingenious, foolproof plan, worthy of James Bond.

We'll just lie to the Navy and the United States Government so I can gain access, under false pretenses, to a high security floating mega-weapons platform, powered by a nuclear reactor.

What could possibly go wrong?

Well, I guess you can see why I am still a bit cautious about names and dates. It has been a very long time, but you never know. At any rate, our purpose was not evil nor nefarious. We were just looking for a fun, interesting adventure. The paperwork was submitted, and, lo and behold, I was accepted.

The date was set. The plans were made. I flew with a friend to Oahu almost a week early to do a little business and have a little fun before meeting the ship. We stayed in a nice hotel and had a nice time. However, in a side story to my side story, my friend had to leave a day early for work, so I decided to save money and stay at "The Y" for one night. Wow, was that a big mistake! I'll tell you this much, I was so tired from the trip's adventures to that point, that I did manage to doze off once, even though the room I had literally crawled with scores of cockroaches, that even saw fit to crawl, in groups, over me as I lay in my not-all-that-comfortable bed. That exhausted slumber was short lived, however, when, as I slept, a particularly large specimen took it upon itself to crawl into my open mouth. No more sleep was had that night.

The next day, exhausted though I was, I drove the little economy car we had rented and returned it to the rental company that happened to be right at the port and met the ship at the appropriate time. After orientation and stowing my gear in the rather bizarre accommodations onboard, B informed me that he had leave to go off ship. Had I been forewarned, I would not have returned the rental car. We went to the rental company, and I explained my dilemma and that, technically, I had already paid to rent the car for the whole day. However, they had already re-rented the little car. All they had left was a fancy white convertible. Oh, Darn! So, two young, wild and crazy guys on leave, were now driving a major cool convertible to find adventure and perhaps romance in Waikiki on a Saturday night!

I had little trouble finding a dance, one with a live swing band for us to attend. The joint was jumpin', as they say, and once I established my dance cred, I got to dance with several lovely, intriguing ladies. Perhaps romance would be found after all. After about an hour or so of just smashing good fun, B said he wanted to go to another place to meet up with some of the guys from the ship. I was game. This had been major fun. Music, dancing, beautiful friendly women with lots of aloha spirit. What other exciting, fun-filled Island adventures awaited us?

Well … None!

B had us go to a bar back near the port. There, we met up with several guys from the ship, none of which seemed to be particularly good friends of his, who were there smoking and drinking and singing very, very bad karaoke. To be honest, I have rarely ever heard good karaoke. I love music and have the highest respect for musicians and singers who have put in the effort to hone their art and their talent. I even appreciate those with modest talent who like to sing just for the joy of it. But I have been over most of this planet, and over the many decades of my entire life I have heard maybe two people singing at a karaoke venue that weren't just plain awful. Why anyone would want to so publicly display their shortcomings is beyond me. Why anyone would deliberately want to endure listening to someone else so publicly displaying these shortcomings is WAY beyond me. But I digress, just a little.

Anyway, you can see that B wanting to leave a fun, friendly venue with food, great music, dancing, and Aloha girls in the moonlight of Waikiki and spend his only night in Hawaii in a smoky, dingy port bar with really bad music, and with nobody in it except the same guys he has been stuck looking at for the past three months, was confusing, to say the least. And we had a seriously cool white convertible!! However, this may begin to give you a bit of insight into the odd duck that was B.

On to the great ship and off to the high seas.

There is no way around it, the sleeping accommodations were odd, to say the least. Big as this ship was, with all of the extra "Tigers" on board, it was hard to sleep over six thousand men, and at least two women. (I'll get to the women later.) Even with the huge bunk rooms, with row upon row upon row of bunk beds, three tall, we still had to share a bed in shifts. I had to stay up late and sleep in the morning, which suited me fine. But another odd thing about it was that, for some reason that I could not fathom, the designers put the bunk rooms directly under the flight deck. Our room was directly under the cable that is caught by the tail hook whenever a jet or other aircraft lands.

All would be quiet until hook hit cable and then there would be a really, really loud, ear-splitting bang, like a cannon going off, followed by a grinding, wrenching sound as the cable was drawn out by the jet with its engines on full throttle, in case the hook should miss, and the jet should have to immediately take off again. This was followed by a loud cranking and dragging sound as the heavy steel cable was dragged back across the deck back into position for the next cacophonous landing. Flight operations would start without warning and continue for most of the time I was supposed to be sleeping. But, still, it was better than trying to sleep at the YMCA!

Flight ops on deck

A carrier at sea is a fascinating place. And, I soon learned, that B was a rather interesting character. He was a natural born schmoozer. He seemed to know everybody, and everybody knew him. Although he wasn't particularly high in rank, he seemed to have full run of the ship, and thus so did I. And so, I did! Our base of operations was the wardroom for B's flight squadron. Between adventures I would hang out in the private chairs of the fighter pilots. Think of Captain Kirk's chair on *Star Trek*, only bigger and more comfortable. The whole thing was like a kid playing Navy's dream. I participated in FOD walks wherein we would all walk in a tight line clear across the flight deck looking for any nuts or bolts or any small objects, Found on Deck, that might get sucked into a jet engine, before the start of flight operations.

Just walking down the hallways was an adventure. They ran the length of the ship, and you would have to step up and through the base of the round edged rectangle shaped doorways that penetrated the bulkheads every twenty feet or so. Looking down them was an amazing spectacle in and of itself, like looking down the center of an endless spring that curved slowly upward and out of sight, following the shape of the keel of the over one-thousand-foot-long ship.

We would hang out on the fantail during flight recovery, with the fierce-looking warplanes coming in straight at us and landing just fifteen feet over our heads.

I personally used a fifty-caliber machine gun to sink one of the countless large trash bags that were constantly being thrown overboard every few seconds throughout the crossing, a practice that I truly hope the Navy has ended.

A fighter lands above

Author "takes out the trash" with a 50 cal.

There was also the extraordinary air show they put on while we were far out at sea. Most of us have seen an air show at one time or another in our life. They are always exciting, filled with fascinating tricks and daring stunts. However, they are always over solid ground and almost always in or near populated areas with lots of homes and buildings and constrained by laws and civil codes. When you are a thousand miles out at sea, on the other hand, there are no such constraints, and the sky is, quite literally, the limit. Oh, I could fill several pages with descriptions of the amazing aerodynamic acrobatics displayed by these hotshot Top Gun flyboys, but that would be too far off the point of the story. I will leave you with just two examples that made use of the surrounding ocean to great effect.

They demonstrated a very impressive computer-controlled gun that is used in defense of the ship that made the fifty-caliber machine gun look like a kid's cap gun. It fired spent-uranium slugs, (they are heavier than lead) at around a hundred rounds in about two seconds. There was a sound, like a very loud, very quick, vibrating burp, and about three miles from the ship a line of splashes shot up into the air forming a long white-water curtain two hundred feet high. It made the fountains at the Bellagio Hotel in Las Vegas look like a lawn sprinkler.

Probably the most impressive demonstration was something that they could never do on land. They would have one of the fighter jets come from miles out and head almost straight at the ship only a few meters above the water, going faster than Mach One! It was spectacular! The sonic blast emanating from the supersonic aircraft instantly vaporized the water in its wake, shooting up a tremendous white rooster-tail towering into the air along its flight path. The sonic boom as it passed, closer to us than I would have thought possible, was devastatingly powerful, and threatened to bowl over everyone on the flight deck.

Another of our favorite on ship activities was hanging out late at night in the combat information center, or CIC. You have all seen representations of it in most movies about the Navy. It's where they do all the tense battle scenes. It's the room with all the cool tech. We'd walk in, (remember, B knew everyone and had pretty much run of the ship) and the room was filled with computer screens. Sonar, radar, planed position indicator scopes, as well as that transparent, edge-lighted plotting board you always see in movies where some movie star Captain or Admiral is charting the enemy position with a grease pencil.

Late at night, CIC was manned by a group of somewhat goofy kids in their teens and early twenties, bored since, not being in a battle, they had little to do, and, therefore, they were a hoot to hang with. However, this was still a serious place. For example, there was one kid holding onto an ax, who didn't move around as much as the others, and he stayed close to a machine covered with a glass top and a lot of knobs. I asked him why, and he told me that the machine was highly top secret and that he had only one job, if the ship had been boarded by the enemy and it was going to fall into their hands, his one job was to destroy that machine with the ax.

View from the Bridge

Overall, the most memorable time spent on the ship was on the bridge. One night, around one in the morning, B and I found ourselves, as we had a couple of times before, once again on the bridge. We talked to the guys, perused the various tech equipment, with which I was already familiar, I sat in the captain's chair, himself not being there at the time, and did general hanging out stuff. Then, B, having not said a word to me, using his casual, convince anybody to do anything voice, suggested they let me take the helm for a while.

Okay now, I knew that B knew that I had been in the merchant marines, and it's true that I had stood as helmsmen and navigator, on occasion, on smaller ships rarely more than two-hundred-feet in length, but, Holy Sherpa Shorts, me controlling a nuclear aircraft carrier plowing through the pacific ocean, at night, with the responsibility for the lives of more than six thousand men, and at least two women, (I'll get to that later) in my hands? Really!? Is there even a possibility they would say yes?

Well, it was B asking so of course they would say yes.

And so, I took up my position behind the great spoke-studded wooden wheel, the wind on my face, a parrot on my shoulder …

OK, that was not exactly the way it was. But it sounded good.

The reality is, I stood behind a box and pushed a little stick!

No kidding. To steer a massive warship, over a thousand- feet long, you push a little stick. The stick, or helm, is about eight or nine inches long and sits in the middle of a small stand about the size and shape of a three-drawer filing cabinet. Just in front of that stands a large compass flanked on either side by two huge iron balls that absorb any stray sources of magnetism, thus giving a truer reading. The truth is the helm was very responsive and yet simple. You have a compass heading and you watch the compass and push the little stick ever so carefully to the left or right to turn the ship to port or starboard, to follow the heading. The hard part is there is a lag between the stick movement and the ship response that took just a little getting used to, but once I caught the flow it was smooth sailing.

Well, I can tell you it was a pretty cool experience. One made even better by the clever manipulations of B. You see, it was nice of the bridge crew to allow me to take the helm for a few minutes, but B kept them engaged in lively conversation so they hardly noticed I was there. At one point the Admiral himself came on the bridge, surprisingly late I thought, giving me no more than a glance and a smile. He went about his business and was soon on his way again. I never hit any icebergs or submarines or whales or islands or anything else to make the story more interesting, but nevertheless I found it fascinating. All in all, I stood at the helm of one of the largest most powerful ships on earth for more than an hour, and, as far as I know, nobody died.

Overall, it turned out to be a fine and varied adventure. And, oh wasn't there something else?? Oh yeah, the two women. One was an officer I got a glance of just for a second near the officer's mess. She was quite young, very pretty, and perhaps the most immaculately dressed person I have ever seen, absolutely shining in her Lieutenant uniform. I wondered what her duties were on board, but never found out. The other came to light near the end of the weeklong transit. Everyone was out on deck as we pulled up to the dock on our arrival at Bremerton, looking for friends and relatives on the dock far below, and waving, etc. I turned and right next to me was someone who came on the ship as someone's brother, who was not someone's brother. Even dressed in men's clothing it was pretty obvious this wasn't anybody's brother. If that wasn't clear enough, the long, thick auburn hair cascading from under the no longer very effective ball cap was a dead giveaway. I'm pretty sure that the navy wasn't fooled either. They just appeared to be gracious, and open to bending a few rules if it contributed to the happiness and well-being of their men and women.

In fact, I've never been much interested in the military in general, but I came away very impressed, with a very positive impression of our armed forces. I have, however, more than once, thought about the two young women I saw on the trip and wondered what it was like for them. I wonder what it would be like for me to be one of only two men alone on a ship with six thousand women, for a week. I can't say as I know how it would be, but I can tell you this, I would sure like to find out!

Ahhh!

So, where were we? What was I talking about?

Oh yeah, flying.

You can sort of get an idea about B from the carrier adventure. He was clever, persuasive, and sometimes totally unpredictable. He also happened to be a licensed pilot belonging to a local flight club that permitted him the use of one of their planes whenever he needed one. It seemed to me to be an amazing deal. I don't know what a membership cost but, at the time, for a member to take out a plane he or she need only pay fifteen dollars and replace any gas the plane used during the flight.

On the night in question, B had invited me and a lady friend to go up for a fly around the city. Having little to do that night, and always up for ride in a small plane, we eagerly agreed. There is nothing like flying in a small plane. The views are incredible. Especially if you are in a high wing Cessna. A low wing plane, where the wing is below the doors and windows and you actually have to climb on the wing to get in the door, will get you there quite efficiently. However, a good deal of your view below the plane is blocked. A high wing plane, wherein the wings are attached above the doors and windows, on the other hand, gives you an almost unobstructed view in all directions below the plane where most anything worth seeing can be found, and those views, especially at night, were oh so worth seeing. B had procured us a high wing Cessna.

Well, I can tell you we were all in high spirits. After completing the outside inspection, we all piled into the plane and completed the pre-flight check. B and I sat up front as pilot and copilot and our companion, who I will simply call E, sat in the passenger seat behind, all of us wearing earphones so that we could better hear one-another as well as the radio communications, although, it seems, at some smaller airports there is no flight controller in the control tower at night. The single engine roared to a start, and we were on our way to a nice adventure.

As we taxied out to the runway, B pointed out the various controls of the cockpit. For those of you who have never been in the cockpit of a plane, it is much like that of an automobile: various dials and readouts on the dashboard, pedals, and the control wheel where the steering wheel would be on the left side where the pilot sits. The most noticeable difference is there is the exact same thing on the right side, where the copilot sits. The plane can be piloted from either side with equal ease, assuming one knows how to fly a plane.

We had now reached the access to the main runway and, after checking for clearance, pulled out, and turned into the wind. B cranked up the engine to full throttle and the little plane headed down the runway rapidly picking up speed.

It was just then that B did one of those strange, quirky things he occasionally does that leaves the logical mind sputtering. However, I could never in a million years have been prepared for this one.

As we roared down the runway, B sat back, let go of all the controls, and said, "OK. You got it!"

The plane is picking up speed.

"What do you mean, I 'got it,'" says I, instinctively grabbing the control wheel.

The blue runway lights are going by faster.

"You're flying the plane. Take off!" says he.

To say I was shocked would be an understatement. Of course, I thought, and said, he had to be kidding. But one look at him, arms folded across his chest, and a crazy, serious expression on his face that I had seen before and knew meant that there was no point in arguing, told me I was in deep trouble.

"I don't know how."

We're going over seventy-five miles per hour now.

"I've never done it before," says I.

I can see the end of the runway rushing toward me.

"Just pull back on the control and you'll take off," says he.

The headlights of the moving cars on the busy road that runs perpendicular to the end of the runway seem to be drawing a line in the sand, so to speak, for me to cross. It's make or break time, and time is what I am out of. I don't know enough about this machine to turn it off, so now it's fly or die. I had watched people take off before, and so have you. In movies and TV shows. I knew that you keep it steady and pull back the control wheel, but not too much or you'll stall.

Having little or no choice in the matter, I let go of fear and apprehension, and focused on the task at hand. With wide eyes facing straight ahead, and a grip on the controls that could strangle a small tree, I steadily pulled back on the wheel. The vibration from the tires, rapidly rolling on the tarmac, gradually lessened until it became as smooth as butter on warm glass, and you could feel the liftoff in your insides as we were no longer chained to the earth by gravity. And not a moment too soon as we glided low over the bushes at the end of the runway, over the airport fence, over the cars whizzing by on the road below, and took off into the wild blue yonder. Well, it was night, so actually it was the wild black yonder we took off into, with only a smudgy red line over to the unusually clear horizon where the sun had not too long before dove into the ocean far to the west.

And, just like that, I was flying up and above the brightly lit city.

I would like to take a moment to describe that feeling, because above and beyond the drama and stress of the circumstances, taking off over a magnificently illuminated landscape at night is an almost otherworldly experience. You seem to be floating over a treasure chest of glowing, scintillating jewels, mostly ribbons of diamonds and rubies, because of the all the cars, but including almost every color that you can imagine. In addition, everything is moving. Not just from the motion of the plane but the cars are all in motion. There are people on bikes, and people on foot walking everywhere, and dogs. You can even see dogs from your high vantage point. You seem to be able to see everything everywhere all at once.

Beauty can go a long way for calming nerves. Almost immediately the stress of the unexpected takeoff drama was relaxed as we gently glided over the busy but beautiful earth below. Flying, under good conditions, is as easy as a casual drive in the open country. I have been handed the controls of a small plane, just while high in the sky, a few times before and since this occasion, always under good conditions and it has always been a great and joyful experience. This flight, once well into the sky, was no exception. Yes, for the next hour and a half it was a pure joy. Flying over here to see this, flying over there to see that, the scintillating, colorful city below, the black sky above punctuated by twinkling stars and fluffy white clouds that looked upside-down because all the light was coming from below. Just lovely.

Sadly, however, what goes up, must come down.

Now it was time to land the plane and, you guessed it, B refused to take the controls. Having me, an untrained person, control the plane through takeoff was madness, but at least going up in the air there is little to hit. Landing, however, is a different proposition altogether. Aside from buildings, trees, houses, fences, and dogs that could be run into, there was the ground. It had occurred to me that when last I had been on the ground, an hour and a half or so before, the ground seemed pretty hard. Flying about, high up in the nice soft air was, so to speak, a breeze. However, pointing this all too fragile aircraft, carrying us three all too mortal beings within it, at that all too hard and solid ground, shall we say, gave all too inexperienced me somewhat of a pause.

You might ask, "Did I argue, did I beg, did I plead?" Yes, trust me, yes, all to no avail. B would give me some verbal direction, but no more. He said he wouldn't touch the controls, and he was true to his word. So, I'll get on with the story.

First, you have to find the airport. As you can see everything, on a clear night, this is no problem. The airport control tower is like a lighthouse with a rotating light. The sequence and color of the light flashes tells you whether it is a civilian or a military airport. How do you know how to approach it? This is also no problem. Even with no person in the control tower, the airport talks to you, not with words but with reactions. You just take your microphone hand piece and click the talk button a few times, and the runway lights up with a sequential array of bright strobe lights zipping alongside the appropriate runway, moving into the wind, the correct direction to make a proper landing. All you need to do is swing around until you align with the flashing lights. Easy Peazy. Now all you have to do is get from high up in the nice soft air down safely onto that very not soft ground. But how does one know just at what angle to head down so as not to come down too early and hit, or too late and miss the runway? How does one precisely achieve that, shall we say, "Goldilocks" angle? Well, it turns out that there are lights for that as well. Alongside the runway are a couple of rather bright lights aimed up at the incoming planes. They can be either white or red, with one set closer or downwind, and one set farther down the runway or upwind. On approaching to land, you want the lights to be red over white. This indicates you are coming in on the correct slope to land safely, as B explained it. He gave me a little saying, "Red over white, you're alright, red over red, you're DEAD!"

So, after slowly lowering our altitude, I clicked the mike and swung the plane around to align with the line of strobing lights, having little choice, I tilted the control wheel forward and began our final decent. Even though all seemed in order, I have to admit I was more than a little nervous. I mean, I'm landing a damned airplane for gosh sake! The lives of everyone onboard, not to mention the lives of any unlucky fools that we might come down on, are quite literally in my hands. And I've never done anything like this before. Not even on a simulator, or even on a video game. This is where it suddenly gets very, very real. All of our lives are hanging in the balance, and hanging is a misleading word, because "hanging" implies something solid to be hanging from. We are just in the air, high in the air, and there is nothing, absolutely nothing but air between us and the very, very hard ground below. I can only trust in my natural instinct and the hope that if I am truly about to do something catastrophically wrong that B will speak up or do something. But down we did go. The irresistible jealous grip of Mother Earth was going to have us down one way or another.

Down and down we went. The unforgiving earth getting ever closer. The lights of the city, once a glittering joy to behold, are now menacingly rushing by on either side of the small craft, but I stay focused on the red and white visual approach slope indicator lights and remembering the saying. I've still got red over white, so I'm alright, right? The plane glides just over the cars zipping back and forth on the busy highway just before the airport, the oblivious drivers blissfully unaware of the potentially fatal drama playing out directly over their heads. I am now nearly level with the lovely blue lights that line the runway, and then, there it is! The VASI lights are red over red! Immediately I instinctively pull slightly back on the controls, leveling the plane just above the runway. I can solidly feel the ground affect that I have heard about.

B says, "Go ahead, land the plane."

"I can't," says I, "the lights are red over red!"

The blue lights rush by outside the windows.

"You can make it," says he.

"But you said, 'red over red you're dead.'"

The air currents close over the runway vibrates the wings.

"It will be OK. Just set her down," says he.

I can now see the end of the runway up ahead.

"Maybe I should take it up again? Fly around and try again? Planes do touch and go landings all the time," says I.

"No, you've got plenty of runway. It's a small plane. You can make it. Put it down," says he.

He is the guy. He is the pilot. Who am I to argue? And so, I eased the plane down the few remaining feet until there was the thump and rumble of a satisfying, if not particularly soft, landing.

We were down.

However, we weren't safe at home quite yet.

We are on the ground, true, but the long runway has now become a short walkway. No, let's make that a very short crawlway, and we are barreling down it at more than seventy miles per hour. A small plane has brakes, but they are not exactly like you might find on a Mack truck. They are mostly designed for slowing and stopping while slowly taxiing about the airport grounds, not this. Reacting with reflexes that I didn't even know I had, I cranked the engine back to an idle, pushed the control wheel full forward to hold us solidly onto the ground to increase friction, and stood on the brakes as hard as I could. The little plane began to slow, but was it slowing fast enough?

I could now clearly see the short, trimmed grasses and bushes at the end of the paved runway, still fast approaching. There is quite a distance of cleared space at the end of a runway, but I am not sure of how hitting it at high speed would affect us. However, I can't imagine it would be very good for the plane. We had already slowed down too much to be able to take off again, so I had little choice but to hang on, persevere and hope my actions were enough. The end came closer and closer, and

I finally, at the last possible moment, slammed the wheel hard to the left. The little plane shuttered and grumbled, and it seemed for a moment the three wheeled plane could tip over to the right but turning the wheel to the left also created just a small bit of lift on the right wing, just enough, it seems, to keep us upright as the wing slid over the grasses at the runway's end and we careened into the side lane and out of danger.

They say, "Any landing you can walk away from …"

Not too long after that adventure B and his flight wing were transferred to some other air base. After a letter or two we lost touch, as happens. For some reason, I never did climb into another plane with him. However, please don't judge him too harshly for this little stunt. Because, after all, he had watched me take control of an aircraft carrier without any particular training and not even break a sweat. And flying a plane is really a lot like driving a car, except you can go up and down as well as side to side. You never know what you are capable of unless you allow yourself to try.

Even so, don't get the idea that I think pilot training is unnecessary. Quite the contrary. Flying under perfect conditions is fairly easy, but pilots have to be prepared for any number of dangerous situations. Like equipment failure, sudden weather changes, fog. And air pockets, oh, air pockets! One of my earliest memories, I think I may have been about three years old, I remember looking down at my parents while stuck to the ceiling of an old four engine prop plane as it plunged fifteen hundred feet straight down when it encountered an air pocket during a pre-jet-age, transcontinental flight. A guy a couple of rows back broke his arm. I could tell you all about that, but that too, would be another story.

Swimming with Sharks

Throughout my life I have had the dubious opportunity to face death head-on in literally dozens of different ways. I have actually been dead four times, so far. Getting there can be a bit distressing. However, once achieved, I've found that being dead is a lovely experience that I highly recommend everyone try at least once. The last time that I met my demise, I was dead for four-and-a-half minutes before they brought me back. I spent the night in the hospital and then came home and worked on the plumbing. I guess you could say that I am not much fazed or frightened by death. However, there were, at one time, three ways to die that filled me with dread. Cancer, fire, and sharks.

Now since fate or chance or whatever, had seen fit to bless me with so many other glorious opportunities to outmaneuver death, it wasn't going to go cheap just because of my fears. Indeed, I was granted the privilege of experiencing each of these joyful offerings in full force, head-on.

One does not have to actually die to have faced death. In point of fact, if you do manage to die, you haven't just faced death, you've succeeded. No, one only needs to be involved in an experience, the most probable outcome of which is death, and have an awareness of this.

So …

CANCER:

It was not so much the dying, or even the potential pain that I feared, as much as facing the long lingering, wasting away, or worse, being drugged into a state of barely existing and watching everyone who cares about you waiting for you to die so they can mourn and then get on with their lives.

Well, I got the opportunity to face all that around the summer of 1979. You see, at that time I was the head goldsmith and caster for what was slated to be the largest, most exclusive jewelry line in the world.

What? Who? How? You say.

I know. I know. As unlikely as it now seems, it is nevertheless true. I had had the honor of learning the fine art of jewelry making from a wonderful old jewelry master named Jack Fox. I had been transportation for my dear lifelong friend Barby, to interview this wise and accomplished teacher, for a high school class of hers. I watched with fascination as he showed her his lost wax tools and how to use them. By the time of her second interview with him, I, on my own initiative, had made a complete set of tools for her, and one for myself. This impressed Jack, and he then and there took us both under his wing and proceeded to teach us all that he knew. We both grew to love Jack, and he became the closest thing to a grandfather that I ever had.

Jack taught me well, and after a few years I became quite proficient at a wide variety of jewelry techniques, especially lost wax casting of silver, gold, and bronze. However, to that point in my life, jewelry making had been just a strong interest, a subject of joy and fascination, not a profession.

One day, out of the blue, I got a call from Jack at my main job, a wonderful high-quality pottery called "Clay Works," where I worked as a ceramic technician for a nice fellow named Dave. This took me rather by surprise because I had no idea how Jack got the phone number, or even how he knew where to find me. Anyway, he was calling because he had an unbelievably fabulous opportunity for me. He told me that a very wealthy and influential woman, who had been a student of his, had talked a certain Japanese corporation, one that happened to "make" sapphires, rubies, and emeralds, into creating an ultra-high-end line of fine jewelry to promote their ultra-high end artificial gems, which were to be set in gold and surrounded with real, natural diamonds. Lacking the technical skills herself, she had called Jack to find a master goldsmith to head up the actual making of the jewelry line.

For some reason, Jack had sold them on me.

Me???

Jack had taught me a lot, and I knew my stuff pretty well, but, *Me*?? I had never thought of myself as a master goldsmith. It had never even occurred to me to think of myself that way. However, Jack assured me that I could handle the job, and if I ever did run into any problems, I could count on him to advise me. And so …

Jack, Barby, and I met with the lady, who I will call B.B., at her home in La Jolla that night. With my knowledge and Jack's recommendation I easily passed muster. The job was mine! I left B.B.'s house so excited that I literally ran right up the side of my trusty old car, the "Crimson Creeper," forever leaving a small dent in it to remind me of the occasion. An incredible dream come true.

And I lived happily ever after.

OK, well about that …

There were just a few difficulties to be dealt with before happily ever after could be achieved.

Firstly, they were on a very tight schedule. They were opening their first store in three months, on Rodeo Drive in Beverly Hills. The next one in Paris, then New York, then London. They needed me to start the next day. That meant going home, working late into the night gathering my tools and whatever into a portable condition and showing up at a new location in a huge industrial complex early the next morning. Fine. However, the real problem was that I already had a job. I had been working for Dave for about four years. He wasn't just my employer, he was my friend, and I was his only employee. He would never stand in the way of such a great opportunity for me, but I couldn't just walk out on him and mess up his business.

Some of "Clay Works" pottery

Simple, I would just go to work for him after I got off my new job for a few weeks until I could train my replacement. And so, I did. The problem was the new job was big and demanding. I would work there for ten to twelve hours and then go to Dave's for another seven to eight.

But hey, I was young, right?

Well things went along, although I can't say smoothly. Dave had trouble finding someone qualified enough for me to train. In addition, the jewelry designs by B.B. were, I must say, not very good. I found them not only unattractive and clunky, but impractical and difficult to execute.

Bracelet … lots of gold and jewels, but don't swim with it

I had a team of three jewelers working under me, all older and in some things more experienced than myself. This was the cause of a little bit of tension. However, I had been very well trained by Jack and that served me well on many occasions where I proved my abilities. One example was the time someone from the accounting department, or wherever they regulated these things, came down in a panic saying there was an ounce of gold missing! The whole place was thrown into chaos, people running to and fro, dumping out drawers, yanking cabinets away from the wall. I just got up from my jeweler's bench, went over to the centrifuge casting machine, swept out the debris at the bottom, melted it in a crucible with a torch, poured out an ounce and a half of gold and went back to my bench without saying a word.

I have to say that I loved the work I was doing. I would spend most of my day at my bench surrounded by piles of glittering multicolored gems, sparkling diamonds, and literally, pounds of fine gold. I would be setting stones and grinding and polishing gold objects, my work apron covered with gold dust. I would joke to people that I would go home with fifty-dollar gold nose boogers! And I was getting **paid** to do this? More than I'd ever been paid in my life?

Happily ever after doesn't always last forever after, however.

I had now been working there about two months. I had finally finished training the new person for Dave, but as the opening deadline was looming, I was now working seven days a week. I've got to admit that I was getting pretty well worn out, when I ran into another problem. One of the guys, who supposedly had twenty years more experience than me, had done something that one should never, never do. They set up a stripping system that used hydrochloric acid to clean up the gold castings, right next to a plating system, that used cyanide for plating gold onto other metals. "So what?" you say. Well, if the smallest drop of one gets into the other it creates hydrogen-cyanide gas. Very, very deadly! I immediately informed the company's hazmat people, who dealt with it and later added a permanent exhaust hood in the lab, but it was too late for me. It only takes something like five-parts-per- million to kill a person. I got around three or four ppm.

I was slammed down pretty hard, but not taken down completely.

I kept working. I couldn't take time off right then or I might lose this great job. However, from that point my health started going downhill fast. I became weaker by the day. I developed a severe strep infection in my throat and the lymph nodes in my neck swelled up like golf balls. My head got foggy, and I ached all over. I kept working on the project until I had no choice but to take off and go to the doctor. So, I went to a young doctor who had taken over his father's practice, the elder of which I had seen previously. The doc, after examining me, looked very grave. He said I was extremely ill and if I did not go into the hospital that night that I would be dead by morning.

In life, a time comes along when you have to make a decision that will totally alter your life's trajectory. A decision that can sometimes mean life or death. In my life these seem to come along semiannually. The choice was this: I could go into the hospital and lose the biggest, most important, most wonderful job I ever had, or die.

Now, I couldn't be sure. I hadn't completely read my contract. But it was possible that if I were dead, I might lose the job anyway. Not much of a choice.

I spent the next week in a hospital bed with an IV in my arm, pumping something like three million units of penicillin a day into me. I lost both jobs. I had replaced myself at Clay Works, and they hired two people to replace me at the jewelry job. I came out of the hospital weak and wobbly. The doctor said that my liver, pancreas, and spleen had all but shut down before the treatment, but were improving. However, there was something else that he needed to discuss with me. I could see that he was very agitated. He told me that I had a blood disease, leukemia, a type of cancer. I knew what that meant, but I asked anyway. He said it was bad. I asked, "How bad?" He told me I had little chance of survival. I asked, "How long?" He looked down at his feet and said, "Two months, maybe six months at most." I said, "I guess I don't have to worry about saving for retirement." He didn't laugh. This had been hard on my doctor too. According to his nurse, he hadn't been able to sleep. I was his first young patient to be dying.

So, there it was, one of my worst fears of dying was now my reality. But ya know, once I had to face it head-on, it wasn't all that terrible. I mean, there were a lot of life's experiences I would rather have had right then, but I didn't feel the dread that I thought I would. In other words, I could live with dying that way, uh, so to speak.

As it turns out, believe it or not, I didn't die, that time. After a few weeks I began improving. The death sentence was lifted. They never could put a name to what had happened to me. It seems that after the extreme exhaustion, the poisoning, and the infection, I was so close to death that my body was shutting down, and the blood cells I was producing were severally deformed, mimicking a form of leukemia. However, for those few weeks, I truly felt like and fully believed I was dying.

FIRE:

I think the most terrifying aspect of dying by fire is the pain of being burned. We have all, at one time or other, been burned. Even a minor burn can cause excruciating pain. I think we all tend to extrapolate that feeling into how it must feel to be more severely burned, and therefore how terrible it would be to die that way. I won't try to go into a description of how horrible I imagine it would be. I am quite sure you have your own horrible ideas about it. I can say, however, that I have had the joyous good fortune to experience rather severe burns firsthand(s), and even first arms.

As a ceramic artist, one of the routine duties is to load and unload ceramic kilns. The primary kiln we used at Clay Works was an old, gas fired, what is known as a catenary arch, kiln. It was made out of heavy firebricks, including the door, which had to be built and unbuilt every time you fired the kiln. Now sometimes we had a quick turnaround before a big show, and I had to unload the kiln before it was cooled. The hottest I ever unloaded the kiln, taking down the door brick by brick, it was 1,000 degrees F. I was going in and out unloading the pots and shelves and my friend and boss Dave made me stop because my hair was smoking. (And we all know smoking is bad for you.) Anyway, sometimes while unloading a hot one, something would fall over onto me and burn me. I received some second degree, and a few third-degree, burns, but I never dropped a pot because of it. What this taught me was that when I got a burn, I pretty quickly went into shock. That lasted about ten to fifteen minutes, time enough for me to get things done. That was followed by thirty to forty-five minutes of extreme Ouch! After that, things would lighten up, and assuming I got some proper care, things went pretty much back to normal with only moderately annoying pain.

This knowledge served me well the time I really got cooked.

My biggest burn happened while attending a college sculpture class. Advanced Sculpture was a much-desired class and hard to get into. However, seeing as I had not only taught at that college, but I had also been attending classes as a student there for more than thirty years, I had a rather high priority rating and could get into any class I wanted. My goal was to learn more about large scale bronze casting. The process was basically similar to the lost wax casting method I used for making jewelry, but on a much larger scale. I eventually achieved this goal, casting the largest poured bronze casting that foundry had ever poured to that point.

Well, it was at this setting, before my melted metal masterpiece, that I had a wee bit of torturous trouble. First, a word about lost wax casting for those who are not familiar with it. To grossly oversimplify it: you create a wax object, attach wax sprues to make channels to let in the metal, coat it with a high temp plaster-like substance called investment, heat it in a kiln upside-down to melt out the wax, and then pour the molten metal into the hot mold. You see, the metal replaces the wax and so, lost wax.

I had developed a technique of making a plaster mold of a clay object I had created and pouring the sculpture wax into that to get a highly detailed head start on the wax model. My only goal in class that day was simple. I needed to pour the hot melted wax into the plaster mold I had previously made. I planned on light work because I was dressed all clean and pretty. You see, I, *yes me*, I, had a **date** that night, a first date.

I had met a wonderful, exciting woman at a grand ball the week before and had achieved the glorious opportunity of seeing her again, so I planned on leaving early. I was in no particular rush, but I did want to get this step done before I left. The rest of the class was in the building, leaving me alone in the sculpture yard. The sculpture yard was a jumble of equipment, an organized confusion, consisting of kilns, foundry equipment work-benches, and supplies. At the far end, over to one side, was a bench with a setup for melting the sculpture wax. This included a few coffee-pot-like metal containers of solidified wax, and a gas stove-top burner to melt it with. I put one of the melting pots on the burner and ignited the flame. What happened next is a bit complicated and confusing, but I'll try to explain it as best I can. It had been cold the past week, so when the last person to use the wax pot finished and let it cool, it cooled quickly. As it did so, it cooled on top first and as the wax shrunk, it formed a spiraling hole in the center, like a little wax tornado. This was to be significant. I had done this operation many times before, but it seemed to me to be taking a long time for the wax to melt. It was still hard on top, with only a little melted wax at the bottom of the tornado. I took a short metal rod to test if the wax was getting softer. It seemed very hard still, so accordingly, I pressed harder. Suddenly, the gates of hell itself opened up!

To explain, the wax, rather than softening and melting as a whole, had been melting and getting hotter at the bottom of the can. The top of the wax had remained as hard as plastic with only a thin ribbon firmly attached to the metal sides. When I pressed down on it, the attachment suddenly gave way, shoving the hard cap down into the very hot molten wax like the plunger of a syringe, forcing the wax up the spiral opening like water out of a lawn sprinkler. I, in the short-sleeved shirt I was wearing, was instantly covered from my hands to my shoulders with searing, molten napalm. Ya know that special kinda feeling you get when your skin is melting away right before your eyes? Well, I do! Just an explosion of pain. The pain signals shot along my nerves and slammed up into my brain so fast that if I had been wearing a hat it would have knocked it off. Thank evolution for shock. That gave me the time and the presence of mind to react. First, I turned off the gas burner. No sense complicating things with a fire. Let's see, what was next on my agenda …? Oh yeah, my arms were burning. Let us have a learning moment. When you get a burn, say from a match or something, removing the fire doesn't stop the burning. The heat you have absorbed continues to cause damage until it is cooled off. This can happen through slow dissipation or, preferably, through some external means of rapid cooling. I, having absorbed a substantial amount of heat and thus was at this moment roasting like a marshmallow over a campfire, chose the more rapid cooling method.

I began quickly taking stock of my immediate surroundings and had, for once, one bit of good luck. It had, in the last few days, rained, a rarity in southern California. All up-turned vessels were currently filled with water. Directly behind me was a sort of half barrel used for catching the used wax as it was melted out of the heating molds. It had about a years' worth of brown wax drippings mixed with who knows what floating around in the water. It had the quite unappealing look and consistency of Asian hot and sour soup gone cold. I doubt that a demented desert dog would drink from it. But hey, burners can't be choosers, right? So, without further ado, I plunged the whole of my arms up to my chest into the noxious mess, and held them there for some time, until I was sure the cold had replaced the hot.

This is where my previous experiences with being burned came in handy. I knew that this one was pretty bad, but I had shock on my side. I had reacted quickly in taking the necessary emergency steps, therefore, I still had some time before the big ouch hit. I really wanted to get this project done, however, I knew what would happen when this incident became known, so I decided to finish the work I had started before going in and reporting the catastrophe. I poured the remaining wax into the mold, cleaned up the work area, put my stuff away, and went in the face the music.

The term "freaked out" would best describe the reaction of each person I encountered, including the teacher. I must admit, I did look like a victim of a major nuclear accident, or war atrocity, and by now I was firmly in the grip of the big ouch. As a result, as predicted, I was immediately escorted to the college nursing facility. Once there, I ran into even bigger trouble.

The kind and competent healthcare professionals had never had such a dire emergency case come into their office. They were not equipped to handle an injury of this severity. They wanted to have an ambulance take me to the hospital at once. But remember, I had an important date that evening. My potential romantic partner, let's call her D.P., was the CEO of her own corporation and very busy. It was purely luck that she had that evening free. And it is often true that if you cancel on a first date, for whatever reason, you seldom get a chance for a second. No, I had to go through with my plans. I couldn't be shot down by a little thing like major burns over a significant portion of my personage. My would-be caretakers were most insistent, however, that I needed to go to the hospital.

After a long, protracted debate, we finally reached a compromise. They would reluctantly let me go, covered in thick gauze bandages from my hands to my shoulders, if I promised that I would go to the hospital. This promise I fully intended to keep.

I just didn't say when.

I managed a quick primping and a rather difficult change of clothing. I was fully out of the big ouch and firmly into the "yeah, it hurts, but what are ya gonna do," stage by the time I was off to meet the lovely D.P. at her ritzy Point Loma home. They say romance is in the eyes, so I must have been doing okay because it was only after she met me at the door, gave me a full tour of the house and we sat together and talked, a full forty-five minutes, that she suddenly looked surprised and exclaimed, "What … did something happen to your arms?"

I must say, we had a great time together. We went out for a nice dinner, window shopped the fancy stores along the street, danced together on the sidewalks, then we went back to her place and, uh, well it was a lovely evening.

It was near midnight when I finally left, but I couldn't just go straight home. Remember, I promised that I would go to the hospital, and I always try to keep a promise. So, I drove to the emergency ward. When I got there there were about forty people ahead of me waiting to be seen. When I got to the window and gave them my card, they asked me why I was there. I told them that I'd had an accident and had burns over most of my arms. It was as though all hell broke loose. They called the emergency team and told them to bring a gurney stat. Suddenly people were everywhere running to and fro in a near panic. Someone asked me when this happened. When I told them, "About two thirty this afternoon," everyone kind of stopped and just stared at me, like I was from outer space or something.

They took me back right away, and once I got into the treatment alcove, I had them call upstairs to where my friend and housemate, a nurse, happened to be working that night and she came down. After the doctor arrived, they took off the bandages from my mangled arms. I've got to say, it was pretty darn gruesome looking.

Now, this is where the real fun begins.

The wax had done a good job of covering my arms. There were large, medium, and small patches of the dark brown wax from my hands to my shoulders, leaving little skin left exposed. The brown patches were ringed with red and pink skin, with areas of white between them where the skin wasn't burned. There wasn't much white. The doctor's job was to try and remove the wax. My job was to endure it. With the help of my nurse friend, he first tried to pull the wax off. Using forceps, he grabbed the edge of one large, thickly encrusted patch and tried to lift it off. It did come off, however, so did my skin, like that of a well-done Thanksgiving turkey. I believe I may have said "Ouch" or something. Maybe something just a little bit stronger. At any rate, that clearly was not going to work. He tried a few other methods with not much better results.

They finally settled on an experimental approach that had some success. Wearing heavy rubber gloves to protect his hands from the heat, he repeatedly dipped a very rough towel in very hot water and vigorously scrubbed the wax from my arms a little at a time. So, I learned if you really want to be clearly aware that you are alive, cover your arms with severe, extremely painful, burns, add heat to them again just to be sure the nerve endings are as fully stimulated as possible, and then have someone sandpaper them for more than an hour. There are levels of pain that are impossible to describe. Suffice it to say that it is absolutely amazing just how much pain a person can endure without going stark raving mad. It is also amazing that we have evolved to quietly sit there while someone is causing us this pain because we believe they are doing so for our own good.

I was in bandages for weeks. The teacher asked me to tell the whole class about the experience. In fact, art and shop teachers had me come into their classes for years to relate the story. It was a great cautionary tale, because, in theory, if it could happen to a person of my experience, it could happen to anyone. It was a humbling and humiliating experience, but worthwhile if it would help prevent future accidents.

I had received some first, a lot of second, and a few third degree burns over a significant portion of my body. Eventually, over the years, the scars faded and became unnoticeable. The doctors made it clear that I could easily have died from the burns that I received, therefore, I have a pretty good idea of my second dreaded way to die, death by fire. You might question my reasoning on going on a social engagement under such dire circumstances. Well, I can only say this: life gives us opportunities and obstacles. If we let the obstacles prevent us from experiencing the opportunities, we will most probably miss out on the best life has to offer and lead mundane, pointless lives. I prefer to take the chance.

SHARKS:

I must say, of the three least favored ways of dying, being attacked by sharks was, and is, the most terrifying of all. It is truly the stuff of nightmares. Unlike cancer or fire, which are probably just bad luck, with sharks, there is something out there with a mind, deliberately stalking you. As FOOD.

And, unlike, say, a mountain lion, that will try to kill you as quickly as it can, a shark doesn't care if you are dead or alive. It will eat you slowly, one huge hunk at a time while you scream and bleed, leisurely ripping you apart with hundreds of razor-sharp teeth. And to top it off, you are not even in your own environment, you're in its. You can't run, or hide, hell, you can't even breathe in its world. In other words, death by shark = very bad.

That being said, I have had many face-to-face shark encounters. Most consisted of myself and a shark that just happened to be sharing the same area of the ocean together. Three, however, come to mind as something different.

The first memorable meat-eater meeting took place one summer when I was not quite old enough to drive. I had headed over to La Jolla, north of San Diego, with my brother, Jim, and a couple of his friends, to do some snorkeling. Our point of entry into the water was a place on the cliffs the locals called "The Clam." It was called that because it was a scalloped semicircle of stone resembling a clamshell projecting over the smaller and narrower of the two entrances to La Jolla cave. The clam sat about forty-nine feet above the water at low tide. In my youth we would go there as often as we could to do cliff diving and jumping. There are few more exhilarating feelings than standing high on that cliff, the sound of the waves crashing over the rocks below, the smell of the salt air and seaweed wafting on a sun-warmed breeze. Gazing down and timing the swells before taking that leap of faith into weightlessness. Of course, it was a fairly dangerous activity, but that's why it was fun right?

I can tell you, hitting the water from that height was like hitting concrete. If you dove, it felt like you would flatten your head. If you jumped, you would hit the water so hard and fast your feet would make a hole in it that would slam shut, just about the time your head was passing water level, with such a *Ka-Whump* it felt like your head was being hammered on all sides simultaneously. However, that wasn't the biggest danger. As I was saying, the cave entrance was in a very narrow passage between two stone cliff faces. The powerful turbulent waves repeatedly surged into the passage and through an even narrower, and highly dangerous, slit into the cave. Even if you avoided hitting the rocks both above and below the water, if your timing was off, you could still rise to the surface only to be caught in a bad in-flowing current and dragged into the potentially deadly maw of the cave entrance where you could be mangled, or drowned, or both. Like I said, it was fun.

Brother Jim on the clam

So, on this particular day, our plan was to jump off the clam holding our snorkeling gear and swim fins, and once in the water, put them on and explore and adventure. Holding onto one's gear through such an impact was no easy feat however, and, as perhaps could have been predicted, one of Jim's friends lost his swim fins. Therefore, before we could get started, we had to find them. We all began diving toward the bottom, about fourteen feet down, and searching. The water was, as it almost always is in southern California, just a bit murky, limiting visibility to about eight feet. So, we had to swim down a ways before we could even see the bottom. I, figuring the current may have pulled them out from shore-ward, was searching a bit further out than the others. On about my tenth dive, I saw what looked like a large, light colored patch of sand. Thinking that it was as good a place to look as any, I began to swim toward it. You can imagine my surprise when it began to swim toward me. As I approached it, and it in turn approached me, I could see, to my alarm, that it wasn't the bright, cheerful patch of gentle sand that I had taken it to be, but that it was indeed that famous terror of the deep, that notorious man-eater, that man-munching monster of legend, a great white shark!

The ocean is, at best, always a place of potential danger. I am now, and was at that time, very aware that there are many potentially deadly possibilities whenever you enter the water. However, facing this particularly gruesome possibility was enough to shake one to the foundation of one's being. As it approached, I could see the row upon row of razor-sharp triangular teeth, made just for ripping and slashing whatever it chose to shreds, in a fixed sardonic grin. I could see the cold, coal-black, empty eyes, the eyes of death itself, turn in my direction.

This was it.

There was no doubt about it.

I was fish food!

This was truly a heart-stopping moment. As mentioned, I was out of my element. There was no outswimming the toothy beast. There was no hiding. There were no "Shark Patrol Rangers" coming to the rescue. There was nobody else around, except the guys I came with. Wait a minute, the guys I came with! They had no idea of the danger! I thought to myself that I might be a goner, but they were far enough away from the imminent threat that they could probably escape to safety if I could just warn them.

I swam hard to the surface and began yelling at the top of my lungs to get out of the water as fast as they could. However, all my warnings fell on deaf ears. Well, not really deaf ears, wet ears. Or more accurately, ears full of water. You see, my comrades were all doing the same thing I had been doing. They were all swimming, masks and snorkels on, with their heads, and ears, down in the water looking for the lost fins. No one could hear a thing I shouted.

This was quite aggravating. Here I am, making a grand, noble gesture as my final act in this world, and nobody is paying attention to witness it!

I hollered and splashed and thrashed about, but to no avail. None of them ever stuck their heads up to hear me. After what seemed like a long time, I noticed something. I wasn't inside a fish. I stuck my face back down in the water to take stock of my situation and, to my amazement, the shark was gone, nowhere to be seen.

Perhaps all my thrashing about dissuaded the shark from snacking just then, but most probably I just didn't look enough like a seal to be of interest.

The next time that I had an up-close encounter with a shark I did perhaps, at least for a moment, look more like a seal. We were once again, my brother Jim and I, at La Jolla for aquatic fun in the sun.

Snorkeling was not our goal on this occasion, we were there to meet dear friend Barby, and her then paramour, Chuck, for swimming around and general cavorting about at the shore. Our location for this summer adventure was a ways south of the clam and La Jolla cove at a beach near what we called seal rock because there were often one or more seals or sea lions sunning on it. Our friends were not expected for another half an hour or so, so Jim and I decided to swim out to the rock. I guess most of us at one time or another, mostly in our youth, had the luxury of time to just make casual decisions about what you wanted to do with your time. For me, that seems like a hundred years ago.

Anyway, we set out for the rock which lay, I guess, around two-hundred feet from shore, a journey we had made on many other occasions. The swells rolled around the flat-topped sloping rock, splashing and foaming, creating roiling currents that we had to swim through to get there. Jim reached the rock first and climbed up onto it. I was fighting my way through the currents, in the deep waters just adjacent to the rock, when something caught me by the leg, just above my right knee. The force of it dragged me backwards through the water for a few feet and I remember feeling a tearing sensation. It didn't exactly hurt, but felt more like ripping cloth. I kicked myself free and continued on to the rock.

Once safely on the rock, I looked down at my leg and was greeted by a most disturbing sight. I had a bright red foot! I then noticed a thin crimson ribbon leading up to my knee. However, it was what was at the top of the ribbon that most got my attention. Just above and slightly to the inside of my knee was a neat row of evenly spaced slashes. Most were less than an inch with the longest just less than two inches. They were not so very deep except near the center of the line, there they got deeper until the very center which was the longest and the deepest. At that point my outer covering had been completely compromised. Looking in through the gaping hole I could clearly see fat and muscle and stuff. It kinda looked like a ham. It was an odd feeling. Standing on a rock at the edge of the Pacific Ocean a person can expect to see many interesting things, but one does not expect to see one's inner self.

I knew it was bad, and I knew that it must have looked pretty bad, mostly from Jim's reaction. Jim was not what you would call a squeamish guy. Once, in our wild youth, when he was practicing shooting, he got hit in the foot with a ricochet. Why, he just sat down and dug the spent slug out of his foot with an ice pick, with hardly so much as a grimace. He was pretty tough alright, but when he looked at my wounds, I honestly thought that he was going to faint.

When I looked at it, three things about it surprised me. One, it didn't bother me to see it. Two, it didn't bleed very much for such a large hole, just a thin trickle. And three, it didn't hardly hurt at all. I don't think it was because of shock because it never did really hurt, ever. There was a slight sting, and that ripping sensation when it happened, but after that, it felt a bit odd, but not really painful. Also, despite the obvious damage it seemed to work just fine. Curious. In fact, the whole thing wouldn't have been all that upsetting except for one thing … we were still on the rock. To get back to shore, we had to swim through about two hundred feet of, what appeared to be, water infested with hungry sharks, and I was trailing blood.

It was a lovely afternoon. The bright summer sun warming our skin that was intermittently cooled by the pleasant salt spray from the waves crashing against our tiny rock island, carried across to us by a gentle breeze. The roar of the surf. The cries of the seabirds. The sunlight glittering on the sea all around us. It wouldn't be a bad place to spend the rest of our lives. And that is just what we would have to do unless we could get across that tiny little couple hundred feet of water. Think about it. What would you do?

We pondered our situation for some time. We couldn't expect any help from shore. This was a long time ago and there weren't as many people around as there are now. We weren't going to be rescued by the navy. We came to the conclusion that we had no choice but to make a swim for it, as fast as we could and both at the same time so hopefully at least one of us would make it. So, we dove in, facing a fear impossible to put into words, and swam, swam, swam like crazy people, and, to our surprise, we both made it, dragging ourselves up through the crashing surf huffing and puffing.

Well, it looked like we'd dodged a bullet. Actually, it looked like Jim had dodged a bullet. I, on the other hand, looked like **I** had taken a bullet square in the knee. We still had to meet up with Barby and Chuck. It was amazing in those days, nobody had cell phones or GPS and still we always managed to meet up on time in faraway places. So, I just stood around on the beach bleeding until they got there, and, I must say, when they did get there, they were a little bit freaked. Chuck, being a "get it done" kind of guy, insisted I go to the main lifeguard station. So, after a long walk to get there, the lifeguards took an also freaked-out look and said they weren't equipped to handle a rip like that, and so I walked all the way back. Again, this was a different time. There wasn't any of this *Baywatch* stuff.

After an otherwise pleasant afternoon at the beach with the friends, we swung by the doctors' office on the way home. Remember when you had "a" doctor who knew you, and you could just "drop by" and they would see you? At any rate, he said, by the time I got there, that the wound was severe but it had been open to contamination for too long to be stitched shut and it would best to leave it that way so it could drain. I left with a clean white bandage that I had to change daily, and I was soon back in the water again. The scar that now remains is only one among many, the physical reminders of other adventures.

Now, finally, we get to the last section of this long, "shaggy dog"-like story about—what was it called?—Oh yeah, "Swimming with Sharks."

A few years back I had one of those "Big" birthdays. You know, one with a zero? My little "Wonder Muffin," Arlene, decided that we should do something really "Big" to celebrate. We settled on a Tahitian cruise! Pretty cool, huh? We even got two very dear friends to go as well. For simplicity, let's call them Fran and Mitch. Mitch's birthday also fell within the timing of the cruise, so it made for a generally festive occasion. I could write a novel about the beauty, the fun, the intrigue and the almost daily adventures we had on that trip, but I'll try to stick to just the one storyline for now.

The ship had arrived in Bora Bora for a two night stay over, giving us plenty of time to explore and adventure. Both Fran and Mitch were fluent in French, the official island language, so negotiating our adventures was easy.

Our first day, we took a taxi ride around the entire Island, stopping at most of the interesting spots. We investigated sun-drenched beaches and bays and lagoons filled with waters of indescribable mixes of turquoises and blues, unbelievably dramatic volcanic mountains and steaming flower scented jungles. We passed modest native houses and hotels over the water that go for $10,000 for one night.

For our second day, we sought adventure of a more aquatic nature. Our Francophile friends negotiated a deal with a local boat owner to take us around the island and on three special adventures. We would visit a moray eel he knew of, pet giant rays, and swim with the sharks, all for a reasonable price. So off we set, on a small, motorized boat, for what would turn out to be quite a day of adventures.

The moray eel lived in a hole in the coral, in about ten feet of crystal-clear water out in the main lagoon. Our native guide pointed it out while we all snorkeled close by. He then did something quite unexpected. He dove down to the bottom and lured the eel out of its hole with a small fish for bait. To our stunned surprise, he then grabbed the living five or six foot long, tooth-filled tube and hauled it up to the surface where he let it go and it swam back down to its lair. He repeated this unbelievably dangerous stunt three times. This was the second special adventure he took us to, following the first which was swimming with the sharks, which I'm not sure that we would have done if it had followed this trick. Particularly not, after we noticed our guide was missing a couple of fingers.

Bora Bora is a volcanic Island of fantastic appearance in the middle of a gorgeous blue lagoon surrounded by motu islands and coral reefs that quickly drop off into deep ocean on all sides. After cruising around the island within the lagoon, we headed out through the main channel toward the open ocean. We then turned south and traveled about three quarters of a mile along the outer reef before stopping the motor and just floating about a hundred yards offshore. The water, still very clear, varied in color from light turquoise near the shore to the deepest, darkest blue where the reef rapidly dropped off into the nearly bottomless abyss. All around the little boat hundreds of large black fish swam, in, I can only guess, anticipation of what they must have known was to come.

Our guide, tall, well built and clad in only bathing trunks that showed off his sun darkened, already brown native skin, stood up, uncovered a bucket of fish heads, guts, and blood, and began throwing it out into the surrounding water. Almost immediately the water surrounding the little boat began to roil and churn as at least a dozen large reef sharks converged on the chum. I had seen film of a feeding frenzy before, but I never expected to be in the middle of one. Dorsal fins and tail fins slashed through the water as the hungry sharks darted to and fro with incredible speed and power. It was truly terrifying to witness. And, at the height of this insane display, our guide casually says, "O. K., jump in."

Now, I have seen many shows about sharks. Some were movies, most were serious documentaries. In most, our brave divers would be lowered in the water, with a few sharks in it, in a huge steel shark proof cage. Rarely, some exceptionally brave adventurer would take a chance by going into the water wearing a full-length steel chain male suit and gloves, carrying a bang stick tipped with a twelve-gauge shotgun shell for protection, while several trained guards watched over him from the boat holding high powered rifles at the ready. We, in mild contrast, were wearing only our bathing suits, with masks and snorkels and, oh, oh yeah, Arlene was also wearing a thin short sleeve shirt to keep the sun off, I guess that might protect against a dozen hungry sharks.

"Jump in!" the man says. This kinda seemed like it could be a plot to get rid of dumb American tourists.

"Jump in!" he says. Really! I mean, there are a dozen riled up "tooth torpedoes," slamming through the water, just looking to commit mayhem, and he wants to put us on the menu? As the dairyman said as he squeezed the last of the moisture out of the curds "no whey." We were a science-minded group and we were not about to just jump in on anyone's word without some empirical evidence. As though reading our collective minds, our unpredictable guide gave us just the proof we were seeking. It was either proof that it was safe, or it was proof that he was a few barnacles short of a pier piling. With a mighty leap, he jumped far out into the water. It was amazing that he didn't land squarely on the back of one of the ravenous ballistic biting beasts.

Well, the sharks continued to swim and so did he, so that only left the four of us to join into the soup. I stood for a moment contemplating my situation. Remember, death by sharks was one of my very greatest fears. No, it WAS my greatest fear. I had met the random shark now and then in the past. I had even been ripped by one, but I hadn't known it was there at the time. Now a dozen or more sharks **were** there, and they were large, and they were in a freaking feeding frenzy! Would I be crazy to jump into such an obviously dangerous situation? Or, would I be crazy to miss out on a potentially astounding experience just because of fear. While I was contemplating these lofty questions, I heard Fran say, in the voice she used when she has made up her mind about something, "OK, I am going in with the sharks." And even before she could act on those words I watched as Mitch just casually dropped in over the side. These are two of the most intelligent people I have ever known. Each of them has a PhD. Mitch is the most cerebral, quiet, bookish person you can imagine. He literally spends almost all of his time in his own personal library writing and doing research. He is the last person one would expect to be first off the boat into a wildly insane thing like a feeding frenzy. And yet …

The others followed quickly over the side, leaving me alone on the free-floating boat. Truthfully, it wasn't fear that made me last to go in, it was that I had been filming the event and had to put away the camera equipment safely before taking to the water. However, being alone gave me a moment to reflect on what we were doing. I had a lifetime of information saying "Sharks bad! Sharks danger! Sharks are mindless eating machines that can't be trusted or reasoned with!" And yet, here I had indisputable proof to the contrary right before me. Here were four people, three that I loved and knew very well, swimming around among the sharks during an actual feeding frenzy, and there were no screams. The sea did not run red with human blood. I was faced with a choice: was I to be ruled by legend or lead by logic?

I slipped over the side into the sea.

The general feeling of the water here on the outer reef was completely different than it was in the shallow waters of the coral lagoon. The steep slope from the top of the reef down to where it dropped off into the dark abyss was displayed like a rainbow of all blues below me. The water was so clear that you could see clearly for at least sixty or seventy feet straight down to the slanting sea floor, animated by the constantly moving sun spangles dancing on every surface. It was like hanging, suspended in warm air, and gave one quite a feeling of vertigo.

It was both freeing and terrifying at the same time. All around, there was a loud silence. From the surf line near the reef shore came the dull rumble of the small waves accompanied by an almost musical tinkling sound, as broken bits of coral were jangled about by the relentless waves. Added to this was the endless array of clicks, pops and buzzes made by a myriad of unseen sea creatures. And yet, it still felt like a hushed silence, for there were no familiar sounds from the world of air above.

My attention then turned to that other small matter, the dozen or so hungry sharks sharing the water with my friends and me. The five of us, including the guide, floated there together in a loose group, mostly facing outward with our backs to one another. Our fierce-faced friends circulated around us in tight counter-clockwise circles. I had the feeling that I knew what it must have felt like to be in a circled wagon train surrounded by, justifiably, hostile Indians in the Old West. Only, instead of sharp, pointy arrows our hostiles had sharp, pointy teeth, and damn there were a lot of teeth!

Arlene faces the tooth torpedoes

The tooth torpedoes continued to swim around us seeking the remaining bits of chum. Sometimes they swam close, sometimes far, sometimes below us, and occasionally even swimming between us. Meanwhile, the unmanned boat slowly drifted further away from us. I felt a growing sense of apprehension until something happened that changed everything. As one of the dumb eating machines swam close by, I altered my gaze. I looked not at the fish, but into its eyes. And, to my startled surprise, it looked back. What I saw was not some dumb, dull-minded thing groping for a meal, but, in the eyes, the mind of an intelligent being looking into my eyes, trying to evaluate what I might be thinking.

At that moment something inside me clicked. We humans are the ultimate apex predator on the land. These sharks were the apex predator in this part of the sea. They had to be pretty smart to survive in their environment. It seemed that they were smart enough to know better than to disrupt what must have been a steady source of food, in the form of chum, provided by the tourist industry. In other words, they literally knew better than to bite the hands that fed them. With that realization, I continued to observe caution, but any remaining fear was gone, and the rest of the experience was pure joy and fascination.

One should not let the pains or abuses of the past define or control us. I suppose that is the point, or perhaps the moral, of these few stories about my most feared ways to die. One should never let fear, even justifiable fear, get in the way of fully living the amazing experiences life has to offer.

No, I didn't get bit by a shark that day. However, later on our tour that same day I did get bitten by a surprisingly toothsome giant stingray the size of a dining room table, the same kind that killed the famous TV adventurer *The Crocodile Hunter*. But that, of course, is another story.

Printed in the United States
by Baker & Taylor Publisher Services